Starting a
High-income
Consultancy

■

JAMES ESSINGER

the Institute
of Management
FOUNDATION
PITMAN
PUBLISHING

The Institute of Management (IM) is at the forefront of management development and best management practice. The Institute embraces all levels of management from students to chief executives. It provides a unique portfolio of services for all managers, enabling them to develop skills and achieve management excellence. If you would like to hear more about the benefits of membership, please write to Department P, Institute of Management, Cottingham Road, Corby NN17 1TT. This series is commissioned by the Institute of Management Foundation.

PITMAN PUBLISHING
128 Long Acre London WC2E 9AN

A Division of Pearson Professional Limited

First published in Great Britain 1994

© James Essinger 1994

A CIP catalogue record for this book can be obtained
from the British Library

ISBN 0 273 60752 9 (Cased)
3 5 7 9 10 8 6 4
ISBN 0 273 60506 2 (Paperback)
5 7 9 10 8 6 4

Photoset in Linotron Century Schoolbook by
Northern Phototypesetting Co. Ltd., Bolton
Printed and bound in Great Britain
by Bell and Bain Ltd., Glasgow

THIS BOOK IS DEDICATED TO TONY REDDING
*A first-class consultant for whom I was
privileged to work at a time when I had
a great deal to learn.*

'Being in business is not about making money.
It is a way to become who you are.'

Paul Hawken, *Growing a Business*

Contents

■

Preface   vii

Introduction: What you can expect from this book   ix

1 YOU, THE CONSULTANT   1

2 PLANNING YOUR CONSULTANCY   26

3 SETTING UP YOUR CONSULTANCY   40

4 MONEY   86

5 HOW TO MAKE YOUR CLIENTS THINK
YOU'RE WONDERFUL   121

6 WINNING NEW BUSINESS   146

7 EXPANSION   165

Index   173

Preface

■

This is a practical book containing practical guidance on how you can make a success of setting up running a consultancy which is geared to generating high profitability and, consequently, a high income for you.

Business is a serious matter, but while I have been careful to emphasise, throughout this book, the seriousness of the endeavour on which anyone who sets up and runs a consultancy inevitably embarks, I have tried to show how this can also be an immensely enjoyable experience.

I have been a consultant for ten years; of which I spent the first five years working as a salaried consultant for other consultancies, while I have spent the last five years running my own consultancy.

All the advice in the book is tried and tested, and stems either from my own experience as a consultant or from observations of how other consultants – both successful and unsuccessful – operate. I firmly believe that the errors of unsuccessful consultants can provide lessons which are as instructive as are observations of the good business practice of successful consultants.

Very little of the advice contained in this book is the type of advice which you would find in a more theoretical kind of business book, or which you would learn on an academic business course. Frankly, I do not believe that business theory is going to be of much help to you when you set up and run your own consultancy. If you are thinking of doing this, what you need – and need urgently – is practical guidance on how to maximise your chances of success.

I would like to extend my cordial thanks to David Crosby, my editor, for his initiation of this project and his intelligent and continuing enthusiasm for it. My warmest thanks are also due to Julian Goldsmith, managing director of Sector Public Relations Limited, who gave me most useful advice in connection with Chapter 7 and who read an initial draft of this book and made many useful suggestions as to how it might be improved.

James Essinger
Canterbury

Introduction:
What you can expect from this book

■

First thoughts

This book is for a special kind of dreamer.

All of us have dreams; whether these relate to the sort of people
we would like to be, the money we would like to earn, the friends
we would like to have, or whatever other objective catches the
fancy of our imagination and yearnings. In your case, since you
are holding this book in your hands and (presumably) debating
with yourself whether to buy it, I believe I can safely assume
that at least one of your dreams relates to the ambition of
setting up and running a high-income consultancy.

If you are content with that ambition remaining forever a
dream and you think that the reality of creating a consultancy
and managing it would be too much like hard work, you will
probably find what I have to say in this book interesting more
as entertainment than as guidance. No harm in that; I am
perfectly happy to entertain you. But if you are only seeking
entertainment and an opportunity to indulge your dreams
without giving them a chance to come true, you are not the
reader for whom I have written what follows.

You see, I have written this book for a special kind of dreamer: *a
dreamer who is willing to take every possible step to maximise
the likelihood of his or her dream coming true.*

If you are this kind of dreamer, I am delighted to make your
acquaintance. Read on, and I will do my utmost to tell you the
practical things that you need to know about achieving your
dream or setting up and operating a high-income consultancy.

And make no mistake, the consultancy business is a great
business to be in. Not only does the consultancy business offer

an almost infinite range of opportunities for you to make a great deal of money from exercising your intelligence, insight, personality and hard work on your clients' behalf, but good consultants are needed – indeed are essential – whatever the prevailing economic situation.

In a time of boom and economic expansion, there will be a huge demand for good consultants who can add to a client's existing success. In a recessionary situation, on the other hand, there will also be a demand for good consultants because clients may not be able to create an in-house resource to carry out a particular function. In Chapter 1 I look in more detail at why clients use consultants, but I hope that this fact of good consultants being in demand whatever the economic situation should whet your appetite right away.

But there will only be this demand for your services if you are a first-class consultant and if your consultancy is an excellent one. Top-class consultants can expect high rewards. By the same token, mediocre consultants and consultancies will never make a good thing out of the consultancy business. I look at this subject in greater detail in Chapter 1, too.

So my principal task is to help you to be a first-class consultant and to start and run an excellent consultancy. On the way, incidentally as it were, I will help you to:

- start and run a consultancy business which should make you more money than you have ever earned before in your life;
- start and run a consultancy business which will make each of your working days very interesting, and many of them positively delightful;
- start and run a consultancy business which will let you enjoy the immense pleasure of working as a free, independent human being;
- start and run a consultancy business which will give you prestige, power, and a vital, living sense of your own value as a human being.

I can do all this for you, and more. But first, you must not only *want* your dream of setting up and running a consultancy to come true, but you must be prepared to spare no effort, within reason, to *make* your dream come true.

If you genuinely want your dream to come true, and if you are prepared to spare no effort to achieve this, you are well on your way to success and, with my guidance, there is every reason why your venture of starting and running a high-income consultancy should be a triumph.

How this book came to be written

Before we begin our journey together, perhaps I can say a few words about how I came to write this book.

For the past ten years I have made my living as a public relations consultant, management consultant and writer. I have written sixteen business books, some of which have focused on how computers can be used in the financial sector, and others which have looked at more general aspects of the financial sector.

This is my first instructional book. Beyond any doubt, of all the books that I have written to date, this is the one which interests me the most.

The reason for this is not hard to discern. In 1988 I began my own consultancy, which I still run today. During the years since setting up in business as a consultant I have seen many consultancies set up by people I know fade and die, with the person or people involved being forced to make a somewhat embarrassed return to being what Pooh-Bah described in *The Mikado* as 'a salaried minion'.

For many such people, the enforced abandonment of the dream of being an independent consultant was at best traumatic, at worst profoundly depressing. For make no mistake, making a success of being an independent consultant and having all the freedom, high income and high status that goes with it is not only a superb dream but, if you can achieve it, an equally superb reality. Working for someone else; working to make someone else rich; taking orders from someone whom you regard (possibly correctly) as less able and intelligent than you simply does not compare with it.

Now, it would, of course, be ludicrous of me to claim that I am a brilliant consultant, simply because I began my business in 1988 and am still in business. Goodness knows, during the years since I began running my own consultancy I have made many mistakes, including some that were so horrendous that I feel ill merely thinking about them. On the other hand, there are certain things which I have definitely had going for me, and these factors probably explain why I am still in business, and still loving what I do. I believe that these factors are central to making a success of a high-income consultancy. I discuss the factors in detail in Chapter 1.

The fact is that I have a passionate sense of purpose in writing this book. During the years since I began my own consultancy, I have increasingly grown to believe that the vast majority of consultancies which fail do so because of fundamental misconceptions on the part of the would-be consultant or consultants about how a consultancy should be set up and run, and I wanted to write something which would assist newcomers to the consultancy business to avoid those misconceptions. I have seen mistakes based on these misconceptions being made again and again, and each time I saw them being made I thought: *'why doesn't someone tell them how to go about things in the proper way?'*

But I was terribly busy running my own consultancy, which is a public relations and editorial services consultancy with clients in the United States and Europe. Ever since I began running my consultancy I have spent about half my time writing corporate literature, pieces of journalism and full-length books.

Then, in the spring of 1993, a publisher for whom I had already written a business book approached me to say that his firm were looking for someone to write a book about starting a consultancy. The publisher had hardly finished speaking before

I knew that I wanted to write this book.

And almost simultaneously, I decided that my book would correct the dangerous misconceptions which so many consultants have when they set up in business. I felt confident that such a work could contain information which would justify the book's price many times over.

Above all, I wanted to write a business book which was full of practical, useful guidance drawn from experience, not theory. I wanted to write a business book *which worked*.

Let me make no bones about it. *If this book isn't significantly more useful to you than any other business book that you've read, I'm wasting your time and mine.*

I admit it: I enjoy reading business books. I tend to read them largely for entertainment, just as I like watching Arnold Schwarzenegger films for the same reason. I don't expect to learn anything very useful from business books, but then I don't expect to learn any profound truths about the human condition from watching Arnold Schwarzenegger films, either.

Maybe it's sad that I regard business books as a source of entertainment rather than useful business knowledge. If you think this, you're right: it *is* sad. What, though, do I mean by 'useful business knowledge'? What I mean by this is: *practical information which teaches someone how to be more successful in business.*

Now, of course, there are business books which show you how to manage technical things such as the drawing up of a balance sheet or the management of the tax side of a business. But that is *factual* information, and you could get it from your accountant or local tax office as easily as you could get it from a business book. Indeed, it would be better if you *did* get it from your accountant or local tax office, because they will give you information which relates to your own personal case, whereas a business book will obviously have to be far more general in its remit. And it is precisely because purely factual general information about business is likely to be of only limited value to you that I do *not* include such information in my rigorous definition of what constitutes 'useful business knowledge.'

I wanted to write a business book that was full of useful business knowledge about starting and running a high-income consultancy; a book that could be used, within reason, as a guidebook to actually making the dream come true. I was not at all interested in writing a dry, theoretical business book which would languish, forever unread, on someone's shelf.

In order to do this, in order to write the book that you are now holding in your hand, I knew that I would have to do more than avoid writing dry theory. I knew that I would also need to avoid certain pitfalls into which, in my view, the *majority* of instructional business books fall.

I believe there are three such principal pitfalls, as follows:

Firstly, too many business books have the irritating habit of assuming *that the reader's sole interest in life is business*, and that the reader is never going to want to do anything else such as get married, have children, listen to music, go for a walk in the country etc. These are what might be termed the 'our reader is an automaton' books. These books forget that the reader is a vulnerable human being who makes mistakes, feels ill, feels lazy and wants to have an enjoyable personal life. As a result, the usefulness of the advice in these books is often questionable because although the advice looks good on paper, it rarely works in the real world.

Secondly, too many business books make the absurd assumption *that other people with whom the reader does business are always going to behave as the reader wants them to behave.* The whole point about business – and this is a point which is behind almost every piece of advice which I give you in this book – is that other people *don't* always behave as we want them to behave. In fact, as we shall see, sensitivity to the needs and priorities of others is an essential attribute of anybody who wants to make a success of starting their own high-income consultancy. There is not likely to be much useful information in books which do not accommodate the need, in the real world, to factor into your thinking the simple point that other people's reactions are rarely predictable. Such books might be termed the 'tunnel vision' books.

Classic examples of tunnel vision books are almost *all* books which purport to teach the reader how to sell. Books which aim to give instruction in the art of selling almost invariably operate on the principle that the person to whom the reader will be selling is either an idiot, or incredibly gullible, or so anxious to part with his money that it's a wonder he got the money in the first place.

Sales books contain reams of advice on how to make yourself appear dynamic, energetic and the sort of person to whom no one wants to say no. Maybe when written down these principles look good, but just try using them in the real world, where people *do* say no: not because they don't find the sales person sufficiently engaging or sufficiently dynamic, but simply because they don't want what he has to offer.

Thirdly, there are those business books which try to convert the reader into 'the ten minute managing director' or the 'five minute millionaire.' Basically I distrust books with this sort of title, partly because I think it is nonsense to pretend that negotiating one's way through the infinitely complex business world can realistically be reduced to following a set of formulaic precepts that can be implemented in a few minutes, and also because I think it an insult for a writer to try to mould a reader into some sort of robotic character who applies the same formulae to any business situation. Business activity, after all, is only a somewhat specialised type of general human activity, and it would be as misleading to pretend that the mysteries of the business world can be solved by applying a set of formulaic precepts as it would be to pretend that such an approach will work when applied to the business of living one's life in a more general sense.

Why I believe this book will really help you

I can almost hear you saying, 'All right, but what makes *you* think that *your* book's going to be any different from the average business book? What makes you think that your book is really going to help *me*?' Reasonable questions, which deserve a straight and honest answer. And my answer is: no, I don't *think* that this book is really going to help you, I *know* it will. And the reason for this is twofold.

Firstly, I am going to assume that you, like me, are a human being, not a business automaton. Of course I know that you are extremely interested in the possibility of starting a consultancy business which will catapult you to a higher income, high status and other very pleasant things, but I will also be taking it for granted that you have many interests other than getting ahead in business, and that you, like me, will have the usual range of human weaknesses, whether these tempt you – on occasion, at least – to do as little work as you can get away with, or to daydream about your lover, or to daydream about someone who you would *like* to be your lover, and so on.

Secondly, I am going to give you *now, at this very moment*, a list of definite *expectations* regarding what you can learn from this book, and I will make sure that these expectations are met.

Here is the list. For succinctness, I have restricted myself to what I regard as the 12 most important things that you can expect to learn.

This book will teach you the following:

1 How to fulfil your potential in business.

2 How to start a high-income consultancy.

3 How to develop a sensible and appropriate attitude towards the financial side of running your consultancy, and in particular how to minimise your overall financial risk.

4 How to develop the right attitude towards doing business.

5 How to make your clients think that you're wonderful.

6 How to be a truly professional consultant.

7 How to win new business.

8 How to promote yourself.

9 How to decide whether you should expand your consultancy.

10 How to expand your consultancy.

Right, let's get on with it.

You, the consultant

Definitions

According to my *Shorter Oxford English Dictionary*, the first use of the word 'consult' in English as meaning 'to ask advice of, seek counsel from; to have recourse to for instruction or professional advice' dates back to 1635. The first use of the word 'consultant' in the modern sense was much later, in 1878. My dictionary gives no specific definition of 'consultant', but equates the term with a consulting physician or engineer 'who makes a business of giving professional advice'.

That is not a bad definition, but for the purposes of this book I would like to suggest my own definition, which contains an element that is in practice essential to the work of a consultant in the modern commercial world. Using this definition, we can regard a consultant as: 'a person who makes a living from providing professional advice to a client that the client is unable to provide for itself or which it is uneconomic for the client to provide for itself'.

The principle that the consultant provides information to the client that the client is unable to provide for itself, is essential to the work of the most successful consultant. And, since the purpose of this book is to show you how to be a successful consultant whose advice is much in demand, we ought to include that element in our definition from the outset.

A successful consultant whose advice is much in demand. That is the key phrase. *A successful consultant whose advice is much in demand.* Memorise that phrase and keep it in mind not only all the time that you are reading this book, but also during all your time as a consultant. That phrase says exactly what kind of consultant you need to become if you want to start a high-income consultancy and run it with success.

Types of consultancy

In the vast majority of cases, the consultant of today provides advice *in a specific area*. I do not regard my job in writing this book as being to suggest in what area you yourself specialise, because – for reasons that should be obvious anyway and which will certainly become clear as you read this book – you ought already to know what your area of specialisation is. No one in their right mind tries to set up as a consultant without some previous experience in the commercial or professional discipline in which they intend to offer consultancy advice. On the other hand, the problem of *how* you ought to go about setting up as a consultant most definitely remains, no matter how experienced you are in your specialisation. This book is designed to help you with that specific problem.

In essence, all business consultancy is *management consultancy*: that is, the consultant gives the management of a central or local government office, public body or commercial organisation, advice about how to run the office, body or organisation more efficiently and/or more cost-effectively. Within that very wide remit, there are numerous opportunities for a consultant to specialise in a very specific type of management consultancy. The following lists some of the main areas in which consultants specialise, and what such specialisation entails. Note that the list should not be regarded as exhaustive, but rather as giving a flavour of the kind of specialisations that are available.

- **Administration consultancy:** advising clients on any aspect of the administration of their organisation, such as office organisation and the implementation of administrative systems.
- **Financial management consultancy:** advising clients on

any aspect of their organisation's financial management, such as setting up accounting and financial management systems.

- **Human resources consultancy:** advising clients on any aspect of their organisation's use of human resources, such as human resource planning and job evaluation and grading.
- **Information technology consultancy:** advising clients on any aspect of their organisation's use of information technology, such as the choice of hardware and software.
- **Marketing consultancy:** advising clients on any aspect of their organisation's marketing activity, such as advertising, sales promotion and public relations. Note that because marketing consultancy offers a very wide range of opportunities for consultancy activity, many marketing consultants specialise in one specific discipline, such as advertising, public relations or sales promotion.
- **Production consultancy:** advising clients on any aspect of their organisation's production activity, such as production planning and quality management.

3

On the other hand, some consultants prefer to remain as general management consultants: that is, they advise their clients on any area of difficulty which may arise. For obvious reasons, consultants offering general management consultancy services require an exceptionally good rapport with their clients which includes a great deal of trust on the client's part.

Good and bad consultants

For consultants, as with so many other areas of human activity, quality is everything. Just as the difference between Frank Sinatra and a tuneless fellow singing in his bath is essentially merely a difference of quality, there is a whole world of difference between the expertise of a superb, knowledgeable and dedicated consultant and a consultant who has no idea what it means to be a consultant and who gives bad advice to his clients. I have already touched in the Introduction on the essential need for an ambitious consultant to be a quality consultant, and now I want to look at this point in greater detail.

I do not imagine that you would have begun reading this book if you had not already been pretty much convinced of the importance of the consultant's role in the modern business world. However, even if you are already convinced of this, I think it important to look briefly at why consultants are needed at all.

The first consultants in the modern sense of the word flourished in the latter years of the nineteenth century, and provided consultancy in the fields of medicine and engineering. Although I have nothing but praise for the skills of the engineers who helped to build those marvels of nineteenth century civil engineering – many of which are still with us today – I do not think I can regard the activities of the medical consultants of the 1880s and 1890s in quite such a praiseworthy light. When one considers the very high regard in which medical consultants were held late last century, it is both amusing and discomfiting to reflect how little they really knew about their subject in those remote times before the discovery of antibiotics and all the other discoveries of modern medicine. This prestige of the medical consultant has, of course, persisted into our own age, although nowadays there is at least some justification for this prestige.

My point here is that, by and large, nineteenth century engineering consultants really did provide some first-class advice to their clients, whereas – on the whole – the quality of the advice which nineteenth century medical consultants provided to their patients was much lower. However, the patients were often desperate, and the nurses and doctors regarded the consultant as a sort of demigod, so the patients no doubt thought that the advice which they were getting from the consultant was first-rate, even though the patient might drop dead a couple of weeks later.

And this dual scenario – in which the consulting world can,

broadly speaking, be divided into those consultants who really do provide useful advice and those whose advice is not really much good but who manage to surround themselves with an aura of authority and ability – most certainly persists today. For every consultant who offers a thoughtful, dedicated service built around providing advice that is just right for the client's needs, there are (I am certain) at least half a dozen consultants who are lazy and pompous and whose advice is expensive and useless. And while, in retrospect, we can see that even the most conscientious nineteenth century medical consultant was dogged by the considerable ignorance of medical matters which prevailed at the time, today's lazy, pompous and ineffective consultants have no such excuse.

If, as I presume is in fact the case, you are thinking very seriously about starting your own consultancy, you will have to face the fact that very many prospective clients who you approach – and perhaps even a *majority* of prospective clients – will have had negative experiences with consultants. The most common complaints which clients level at consultants are:

5

- the consultant overcharged them;
- the consultant's advice was less useful than the consultant had led them to believe it would be;
- the consultant's advice was of no use at all;
- the consultant wasted too much of his time – time for which the client was paying – in learning about the client's business;
- the consultant was pompous and pretentious;
- the consultant didn't keep them informed of how things were going;
- the consultant's written reports were wordy and vague.

Guarding against these complaints is absolutely fundamental to good consultancy practice.

The rationale for using consultants

I ended the last section by listing the most common complaints which clients level at consultants. It is essential that you bear these complaints in mind when setting up a consultancy which has the specific aim of becoming successful and generating a high income for you. However, it is also true that the client-consultant relationship – if properly managed by the consultant, and if infused on the consultant's part with energy, hard work and resourcefulness – can be a highly productive one which brings both the client and the consultant considerable benefits. These benefits will stem from the rationale for the client's use of the consultant. This rationale is based on the following principles:

1 *A disinterested observer often sees things which are not clear to those on the inside.*

As a consultant, you are a disinterested observer in that you should be entirely impartial when you view a situation or dynamic in connection with which you are consulting. Being *disinterested* means having no personal axe to grind in relation to the matter on which you have been asked to focus your attention – in other words, that you are cut off from the political aspects of the decision. It does not mean that you are *uninterested* in the matter, because of course you won't be much use as a consultant if you do not find your work interesting.

I do not exactly know why a disinterested observer almost invariably has a better perspective on matters than people who are more closely involved with the problem under discussion. I can only suppose that when people are very closely involved with a problem they are unable to retain much of a sense of proportion or objectivity. Whatever the reason, the simple fact is that, as a disinterested outsider, you will find that you are very frequently able to provide insights and advice which the parties involved are unable to provide.

2 *An outsider is not afraid of saying what he or she thinks.*

However much a corporate body tries to convince its employees – and itself – that it is an extremely reasonably-minded organisation which is primarily concerned with the personal development of its staff, the fact remains that the main aim of any commercial organisation is to make a profit, and woe betide any employee who, even for an instant, gets in the way of that all-important objective.

The result of this is that almost all corporate employees modify their behaviour – and in particular hold back any overt criticism of their corporation – in order to minimise their chance of getting fired. The trouble is that this lamentable situation means that underlings are very reluctant to criticise their bosses, even when the boss has made decisions which any outsider would regard as utterly foolish.

An external consultant, on the other hand, has no such fear of the sack and will not be afraid to say what he thinks. The consultant has the opportunity – indeed, has the *duty* – to be completely objective in the advice that he bestows. And if one consequence of providing that advice means that one or more of the client's directors are relieved of their positions, then so be it.

Of course the objection might be raised here, 'Well, that sounds all right in practice, but what consultant would dare suggest that one or more of the client's directors were behaving in such an irresponsible way that they should be dismissed?'

The answer to this is that while I freely concede that the number of cases in which a consultant would need to advise a client to dismiss directors or senior managers is very few, no consultant worth his or her salt should baulk from this task, if it is necessary. And no client who was worth having as a client would dispense with the services of a consultant, or refuse to pay the consultant's fee, merely because *after careful and thoughtful deliberation* the consultant concluded that the best interests of the corporation would be served by dismissing certain directors or senior managers.

Unfortunately, there are occasionally those clients who are foolish enough to believe that the main reason for using a consultant is to obtain an authoritative third-party recommendation for doing something that the client badly wants to do. When, as often happens, the consultant's advice is precisely the opposite (or, at the very least, differs widely) from what the client hoped, the client will sometimes get very irritable and start directing all sorts of irrational accusations at the consultant. Since it is rarely possible to be absolutely certain that a client will not behave in this manner, the only way for a consultant to protect himself is to ensure that one single client does not constitute too large a part of the business. Because, believe me, if you allow yourself to lose your objectivity as a consultant, you can no longer describe yourself as a consultant in anything other than in name. And one of the most essential things to remember when working as a consultant is that those of your clients who are worth having as clients will only respect you if you strive to tell them what, after due consideration, you really think, not what you think they want to know.

3 It may be impossible for the client to gain access to a specific advanced level of skill other than by using the services of a consultant.

When someone has attained a high level of expertise, they will – unless they have a particularly charitable frame of mind – wish to dispense that expertise for as much money as possible. In most cases it is likely that they will be able to make far more money from that expertise by offering themselves as consultants rather than by seeking to work on a salary for a particular organisation. For this reason many clients have to face the fact that high levels of expertise will only be obtainable from a consultant or consultancy.

4 It is often more cost-effective for a client to use an outsider to provide a special skill which is only infrequently required by the client.

For many clients this rationale constitutes the economic basis for using the services of a consultant. Quite apart from the benefits, discussed above, of disinterested objectivity, willingness to speak one's mind and access to advanced skills, there can be a very fundamental financial benefit of using a consultant. This benefit stems from the fact that the high expense which a corporation will inevitably incur when it sets up a new in-house management function makes it advisable for the corporation to use instead the services of an outsider if the new management function is only required on an occasional basis. Sometimes a large corporation will get around this problem by offering the services of the department to other corporations on a commercial basis, but the basic fact of it being uneconomic for a corporation to create a specialist in-house department where the corporation does not have enough specialist work to keep that department fully employed at all times, still remains.

For example, a corporation which wants to increase the amount of coverage which is accorded to its activities in those newspapers and journals read by its existing and potential customers may decide to set up an in-house public relations function. The cost of setting up such a function would be based around the following:

9

- costs of recruiting staff and/or retraining staff;
- salaries of staff (including related payments such as pension contributions and government insurance contributions);
- costs of office space (and note that even if existing office space is being used, there will still be the opportunity cost of not being able to devote this space to another function);
- costs of office equipment;
- ongoing expenses incurred in running the new in-house department (e.g. costs of stationery, postage, telephone calls, fax transmissions etc.);
- additional insurance costs.

These fixed and ongoing costs can be so high that it rarely makes sense for a corporation to set up an in-house department to provide a function that is not essential to the organisation's operation. On the other hand, using a consultant to undertake this function gives the organisation a very high level of flexibility, as it can decide exactly how much it wants to use the consultant. Likewise, the cost of the consultant's input can be rigidly controlled, whether the consultant is working on an ad hoc (i.e. project-based) basis or on a regular (i.e. retainer) basis. When using the consultant, the cost of undertaking the function will simply be the consultant's fee, plus any out-of-pocket expenses that are agreed beforehand. Unless the organisation completely mismanages its use of the consultant, the cost of delegating the occasionally-required function to the consultant will inevitably be much lower than the cost of setting up and running an in-house department to undertake the function: a course of action which will also be extremely wasteful if the function is indeed only occasionally required.

10 Similarly, where an organisation wants to test out a particular new aspect of functionality, or to initiate a pilot scheme of some kind, it is almost invariably much cheaper to use consultants to do this rather than to recruit salaried staff to carry out the experimental function. This is because it is usually much less expensive to 'pull the plug' on consultants rather than salaried staff if the organisation decides not to proceed with the experiment. There are also ethical issues here, which are not trivial in this age when corporate organisations take considerable trouble over how they present themselves to the public. No reputable corporation wants to be seen as a 'hire and fire' business.

The rise of the 'hands-on' consultant

Although the dictionary definition of a consultant that I quoted at the beginning of this chapter focuses on a consultant's role in providing advice, if you imagine that you will be able successfully to set up a high-income consultancy which *purely* provides advice then you are in for a shock. In most cases, the successful consultant of today must also be a 'hands-on' consultant: that is, he must either be able to undertake the actual implementation of the recommended action, or must have access to people (the consultancy's employees, most likely) who will undertake the implementation.

A principal reason for the rise in demand for consultants who make recommendations *and* implement those recommendations, once the client accepts them, is that since the early 1980s the business world has become much more hard-headed, informal and results-orientated than it ever was before. One result of this is that client organisations are often impatient with consultancy advice that does not come with an ability to implement the advice, once the client is happy with it. There is a breed of consultants known somewhat facetiously by clients as 'seagull consultants' because they drop the client's report from a great height and then fly off! No consultant worth his salt will want to gain a reputation for delivering a report to a client and then leaving the client to sink or swim.

11

Having said that, there is no hard and fast rule here; a few consultants continue to provide purely strategic advice and do very well from the provision of this. But by and large the consultants who do so are working within large and very well-known management consultancies which, I must admit, I often believe are used by large, prosperous client organisations simply so that the organisation can *feel* that it is doing something about a problem, rather than because the organisation genuinely wants to rectify the problem.

Certainly, as someone who is thinking of starting a high-income consultancy, you have got to face the fact that you will almost certainly greatly reduce the chances of making your consultancy a success if you do not offer a hands-on service in addition to an advisory service.

Another factor to consider here is that where strategic advice is unsupported by effective implementation it is all too easy for the client to implement the strategic advice ineffectively, and then, when things go wrong, regard the strategic advice as being wrong, rather than the implementation.

Besides, if your excellent advice has won support and interest from your client, why should you give the valuable implementation business to someone else?

Personal factors which will maximise your likelihood of succeeding as a consultant

So far in this chapter I have aimed to give you a brief, very general initiation into what makes the consultancy business tick. It is now time to make the discussion more personal and to focus on you and your own aims of starting a high-income consultancy.

12   As I mentioned in the Introduction, in this book I do my utmost to give you the practical advice which I passionately believe you will need in order to make a success of starting your own consultancy. However, I obviously can't *make* your consultancy a success, any more than I can make you work hard on your consultancy one evening instead of watching some garbage on television. I can also give you the benefit of what I myself have learned as a consultant since 1988, and in particular I hope I can help you to avoid the mistakes I have made. The advice in this book has been won at the expense of a good deal of heartache and a fair amount of wasted cash.

I will come onto your own motivations for wanting to start a high-income consultancy in a moment, but in the meantime I want to look in detail at the personal factors which I believe will greatly influence your chances of achieving success in running your own high-income consultancy.

I believe there to be five principal personal factors, as follows. I freely admit to having extrapolated these from my own experience of setting up a reasonably successful consultancy, but all the factors are backed by observations I have made of the personalities of other successful consultants.

First, I have never really liked working for someone else.

Second, the two disciplines in which my consultancy has specialised – providing public relations and editorial services for organisations in the banking and high-technology industries – are areas which interest me a great deal.

Third, I have learnt to learn from my mistakes.

Fourth, I am prepared to work any amount of time in order to make a success of what I do.

Fifth, I fear boredom more than worry.

Okay, now to the crunch. *I firmly believe that it is possible to generalise these five factors and to assert that you can start and establish a successful high-income consultancy if you honestly consider that the following apply in your own case:*

13

1 You passionately want to run your own business, rather than work for someone else.
2 You are genuinely interested in whatever professional discipline or specialisation will form the basis of your work as a consultant.
3 You are *genuinely* able to learn from your mistakes, which is *not* simply the same thing as being able to admit that you can make mistakes.
4 You are prepared to work whatever hours you need to work to make your consultancy successful, and those close to you – and particularly those with whom you live – are supportive of this.
5 You fear boredom more than worry; that is, given the choice, you would rather be worried than bored.

To be frank, if *at least two* of the above five factors do not *already* relate to you, you would be very well advised to think seriously about whether you have got what it takes to start a high-income consultancy. I don't think you need worry if *only* two of the five factors relate to you; after all, you should be prepared for a situation where the adventure on which you are about to embark may, like any adventure, modify parts of your personality. In other words, you will have the opportunity to 'grow towards' the other factors as you develop as a consultant and business person.

By the way, if none of the factors apply in your case there's no reason at all why you should regard yourself as some sort of failure! All I'm saying is that I truly believe that in order to make a success of running a consultancy you need to have some basic aptitude, and the five factors above are my suggestions for the basis for this aptitude.

In relation to the first factor (*You passionately want to run your own business, rather than work for someone else*) you should remember that you are not *obliged* to become an independent consultant. No one is going to point a finger at you in the street and say, 'What a pity you never became an independent consultant'. Millions of people are perfectly happy working for other people, and indeed there are numerous activities where, if you wish to pursue the activity, you have little choice but to work for others. If your passion in life is charity work, or running the planning department of your local council, or supervising a heavy industry's production line, you may not have a chance to indulge yourself unless you are prepared to be an employee, although it has to be said that consultants are arising in all sorts of sectors – such as broadcasting, for example – where it was previously the norm for participants to be salaried employees.

Besides, there is plenty to be said for being an employee. Your fellow sufferers are all around you, and no doubt you can befriend some of them. You can use the telephone in your office and switch on your radiator with little fear that you will be asked to contribute towards the telephone or heating bill. And then, of course, there is the nicest thing of all about working for other people: at the end of every week (or month) you receive a regular wage or salary payment. Believe me, you will miss your salary when you set up your own consultancy, particularly during the first few months.

Moving onto the second factor (*You are genuinely interested in*

14

whatever professional discipline or specialisation will form the basis of your work as a consultant) many people find their work slightly – or, even, very – boring, and are happy with a life where they obtain their principal satisfactions from their leisure pursuits. Nothing wrong with that. But if you are that sort of person; if you regard work as something to be tolerated rather than as the centrepin of your whole existence; you *may* need to forget about starting your own consultancy. On the other hand, you may simply be in the wrong job, but make sure you find a discipline or specialisation that you really *do* like before you start to think seriously about becoming an independent consultant in that discipline or specialisation.

Now onto the third factor (*You are genuinely able to learn from your mistakes . . .*). Sadly, many people make the same mistakes over and over again, and never learn from them. I don't know exactly what the recipe is for learning from your mistakes, although certainly a large part of this is having the courage and humility in the first place to admit that you *have* made a mistake. Once you've done that, you need to say to yourself, 'Right, well, that was pretty stupid, wasn't it? I'm not going to do that again.'

15

Yet, how few people really have the courage and humility to admit their mistakes! So many people love to live cocooned in a little shell of conceit and absurdly unjustified self-confidence. A public relations consultant I once worked for was just like this. He once actually said to me, 'James, I'm right 99 per cent of the time,' and I am sure that he was still believing this even as the consultancy which he had formed lurched from one financial crisis to the next. If you think you're right most of the time, you may well be too much like this fellow to make a success of running your own consultancy.

Now onto the fourth factor (*You are prepared to work whatever hours you need to work to make your consultancy successful*).

How hard are you prepared to work? Even if your honest answer to this question is, 'not very', that's certainly nothing to be ashamed of. If you are able to make a good living by working during the day and having your evenings and weekends off, then good luck to you. But if you are the sort of person who not only likes to have evenings and weekends free, but insists on this, then forget about setting up your own consultancy.

Finally, there's factor five (*You fear boredom more than worry . . .*).

Again, you must be honest with yourself. Putting it bluntly, do you fear worry more than boredom, or boredom more than worry?

I have often suspected that the human race divides neatly into those who are prepared to tolerate any amount of boredom if they can avoid worry, and those for whom exactly the opposite is true. Again, it is not for me to make a judgement on which of these two types of personality is 'better': especially since the notion of one personality being 'better' than another is pretty absurd. On the other hand, it is extremely unlikely that anybody who genuinely and consistently prefers boredom to worry would be temperamentally suited to making a success of running their own consultancy.

If you have looked through the above five points and have decided, with honesty, that all five – or three or four – can be applied to you, then welcome aboard, because we are going to have a great deal to say to each other. But even if – and I want to repeat this point because it is extremely important – you conclude that only a couple of points can be applied to you, I'd say that you may still be a contender for starting your own high-income consultancy. After all, your own self-assessment may not be entirely accurate. And as I say, you must reckon with your personality developing if and when you become an independent consultant.

If you are truly and utterly committed to becoming an independent consultant, you will have a chance of success even if you are forced to conclude that only one of the above factors applies to you, or even that no factor does. If you have never set up your own consultancy, for example, you will probably not know what capacity you have for blisteringly hard work, just as if you have always worked for someone else you will probably not know what your own worry threshold is. Yes, I do believe that the five factors discussed above are useful guides to assessing your own aptitude for making a success of setting up your own high-income consultancy, but equally I believe that *if you are truly motivated to making a success of running your own high-income consultancy, that motivation will give you the energy and willingness to develop your own personality along the lines that are required to make you successful.*

More on motivation in a moment. As a sort of appendix to the five success factors, I ought finally to say a few words about the health factor.

Working hard is not the same – indeed, is definitely not the same – as running round in frenetic fashion. Working hard is much more a matter of *thinking* hard, and then making sure that you put the hours in to get done what needs to be done. In my own case, I have always made stringent efforts to keep fit for precisely this purpose. However, I do not believe that in order to start and run your own high-income consultancy you need to have a first-class physique and no health problems.

17

On the other hand, I really cannot advise you to try to start a high-income consultancy if you have significant health problems. The emotional and physical effort involved in starting your consultancy is likely to make your health worse. All the same, if you have a health problem that makes it difficult for you to work nine till five outside your home, I do not want to discourage you from starting a consultancy. I am aware that one of your motivations for doing this may be the idea of working at home and on your own terms. Nor do I wish to put you off starting your own consultancy if you have a handicap.

For people who are unfit, I strongly recommend that you make an effort to get fit before starting your high-income consultancy. If you smoke, stop smoking if you can. Smoking is nothing more than slow suicide and besides, in the present anti-smoking climate in business, you will not be doing yourself any service at all if you go along to meet prospective clients and ask for the ash-tray. If you're overweight, try to shed a few pounds. Face the fact that many of your prospective clients – the very clients who, if properly nurtured, can make you rich – may have a mental image of consultants as being fat, fairly idle people who send in whacking great invoices. Your job, from the outset, is to give your clients a picture of a consultant as a hard-working, commercially astute, helpful person who assists them to make their business even more successful than it already is.

Besides, why not make your decision to set up your own high-income consultancy a new beginning in every respect? You are planning to effect a decisive change in your career; why not combine that with a decisive change in your own lifestyle? Get fit, get slimmer, get in touch with yourself. Because the basic fact is that what will ultimately make your own consultancy a success or a failure is your own personality. Remember this and never forget it: *personality, coupled with ability, is what wins clients for consultants*. True, there are some consultants who think that extravagant promises and boasting will win accounts, but even where wordy pomposity does win accounts, it won't keep them.

Motivation

Now let's look at what motivates you.

Pull out a piece of plain paper, and make a list of the factors which you believe are motivating you to start your own consultancy. Done it? Okay, now place that list somewhere where you can easily read it while you are sitting at your desk. During the first months of your business activities as a consultant, you will need to have your basic motivations on view at all times. You won't want to forget them.

What do I think of the motivations that you have written down? Even if I could see them, I would want to be cautious about commenting on whether or not I thought that your motives were valid. The great English barrister Norman Birkett (later Lord Birkett) observed in a famous trial of the 1930s that the motive for a particular criminal's actions was locked in the criminal's own heart. And what is surely often true of criminals is also true of all of us. We frequently do not know exactly why we do something; quite possibly we would be at a loss to explain our true motives. It is usually good enough for us to know that we badly want to do something, and then we go ahead and do it. We are not like characters in novels or films, who do things for very clear reasons.

This being the case, the following comments on *possible* motives which you might have for setting up your own high-income consultancy are only intended to help you to look at your own motivations more clearly. There is no reason in the world why you need to agree with my comments, nor why you should regard my list of possible motivations as exhaustive.

So here's my list.

AMBITION

This is a word which means very different things to different people. How exactly you rank it in your own list of motivations will probably depend partly on how you perceive the success, or otherwise, of your business career to date, and on who your role models are. Where you live is also a factor. In the United States, for example, ambition is usually seen as something of profound importance. When Ronald Reagan was President, he even coined a slogan 'Be All You Can Be' which means about the same as 'Indulge Your Ambitions'. In other cultures – such as Eastern Europe prior to the liberalisation of the early-1990s – personal ambition was something that you tried to conceal, if you had it. Nowadays, with the restrictions of communism having been blasted away in Eastern Europe by the hurricane of freedom, ambition is again something to be proud of in Eastern Europe, and for many people the one thing that is sustaining them through the turbulent and, in some cases, bloody, transition to a free way of life. Of course, both in

19

America and Eastern Europe, the word 'ambition' is practically synonymous to some people with 'motivation', and simply means that they want to . . . well, be all that they can be.

DESIRE FOR INDEPENDENCE

Even if you do not have much idea, at present, of what running your own high-income consultancy will be like, you probably imagine that the freedom and independence to live as your own boss, and to place your own destiny entirely in your own hands, is one of the major attractions of setting up your own consultancy.

It is, too. And while you will have to face the fact that, in the absence of a boss, your bank manager and your clients become, in effect, a sort of series of mini-bosses, this is a far cry from having to listen to the whinings of someone who irritates you but who happens to have you in the palm of his hand because you are working for him (or her).

But there is a catch. You can only have your independence and freedom if your consultancy succeeds, which means if it makes money.

LOVE OF YOUR SPECIALISATION

This motivation, while nothing like as glamorous as the others in this list, is essential if you are going to make a success of your high-income consultancy. After all, at some point, once you have won your first clients and negotiated a contract, you are going to have to sit on the soft thing below your back and get down to some good hard work. If you don't enjoy that work for its own sake, I don't see how you can be successful, and indeed I would question whether you really wanted to achieve success as a consultant in that specialisation, anyway.

MONEY

Only the very rich, the deeply religious, the untruthful or the

20

very foolish say that money doesn't matter, but even when somebody is honest enough to admit that the acquisition of money is an extremely important element of their personal happiness, what they really mean by this is probably that they want to earn as much money as they can by doing something that they *want* to do. Few of us, for example, would be prepared to sacrifice a limb for one million dollars.

The point is that you have every right to expect your consultancy to earn you more money – possibly significantly more money – than you are earning at present. Indeed, money is so important an element of setting up your own consultancy that it requires an entire chapter in this book, and gets it (Chapter 4). However, it is dangerous for money to be your *only* motivation, as you will only earn that money if you have a genuine love of your consultancy specialisation for its own sake (see above).

The great man of letters Doctor Samuel Johnson said that nobody but a fool ever wrote for anything but money, but he rather took it for granted that a man of letters would love to write. You will probably only be successful if you can take it for granted that you love your specialisation.

POWER

If you can make a success of your own high-income consultancy, you are unlikely to be disappointed about the power that this brings you to live as you want to live, and to get people to do (within reason) what you want them to do.

PRESTIGE

Consultants often have a high prestige in society, and if you make a success of your consultancy you are also unlikely to have any complaints about the prestige that your success brings you. True; some people regard consultants as overpaid, pompous and ineffective, but, as we have already seen and as we shall be seeing throughout this book, your job is to prove that you are not like that.

I expect that your own list of motivations will include at least some of the motivations that I have listed above. Whether it does or doesn't, I don't think anybody else but you can expect to be privy, or to evaluate, the motivations behind the major decisions in your life.

Having said that, there are certainly a few *dangerous* motivations, any one of which, or a combination of which, it could be most risky to adopt as the *sole motivations* for starting a consultancy. In my view, the three most dangerous motivations, in ascending order of danger, are as follows:

DISLIKE OF YOUR CURRENT JOB

Let us both be completely clear about this: the fact that you dislike your current job is not *at all* a reason, in itself, to set up as a consultant. Dislike of your current job is a reason to try to find another job that you don't dislike.

If you dislike your current job, ask yourself whether what you dislike are external things such as the journey to work, the environment in which you are working and the people with whom you are working, or the sheer activity of the job itself. If what you dislike are basically external things, you may simply be better off doing a similar job in a different environment.

If you dislike the sheer activity of the job, I would certainly not advise you to become a consultant in that activity.

REDUNDANCY

While I do not doubt (and in fact I know) that a good many successful consultancies have been formed by people who have been made redundant, starting a consultancy merely because you have been made redundant and have no immediate prospects of further employment is not only a very bad idea, but potentially a very dangerous one.

The first danger is that you might simply be better off working for someone else, and if you start a consultancy you will (presumably) be devoting time to running your consultancy which might be better spent on looking for a new job. Equally, if you start your consultancy and don't make a success of it you will have an embarrassing hole in your curriculum vitae which will need explaining or fudging. This danger applies to anyone who starts a consultancy, of course, but they may be better motivated than you and may not have any wish to return to the world of salaried work.

The second danger is that you may waste your valuable redundancy money on setting up your consultancy. In this book, the method which I am recommending for forming a consultancy will involve you in minimal expenditure and minimal financial risk, and in fact – for reasons which I will explain – I regard investing too much money in your consultancy upfront as a positive mistake. So if you decide to blow your redundancy money on setting up your consultancy, you will not only be cheating yourself, but also disregarding my advice.

23

The third danger is that, being redundant, you will probably have fewer existing business contacts than you would have if you were working, and as you shall see, existing business contacts are an important part of setting up a high-income consultancy successfully.

The final danger – and probably the most significant one of all – is that, being redundant, you are already in a negative frame of mind. When you are setting up your own consultancy, the last thing you want to be in is a negative frame of mind.

FINANCIAL DESPERATION

This is without any doubt the worst motive of all for setting up a consultancy.

If you are financially desperate, you will not – not even if you are a very good actor – be able to conceal this from your potential clients, and from people (such as bank managers) who may be sources of any finance that you may need in setting up your consultancy. As you will see a little later in this book, you will not necessarily need to borrow money in order to set up your consultancy, but if you decide to, you certainly do not want to be desperate about it.

If your experience of the business world has not already taught you that people want to do business with winners, not losers, and that any indication that you are financially desperate is going to put off your potential clients as surely as if you went to a formal meeting with them dressed only in your under-clothing, get wise. Desperation does not attract, but repels, and if you imagine that your potential clients will feel sorry for you and give you their business to help you out, you're dead wrong.

24

Similarly, bank managers or other professional sources of finance do not lend money to people who they perceive to be financially desperate (and this is something which they are trained to perceive). In fact, bank managers and other sources of finance much prefer to lend money to people who do not need it. Yes, I know that this is unfair and rather absurd, but that is how they operate. Of course, it is pretty easy to work out why bank managers and other sources of finance much prefer to lend money to people who are already financially well off.

If you are currently financially desperate, there's no reason why you shouldn't start your own consultancy *once you have made every effort to stabilise your financial position*. The best way of doing this is to force yourself to look calmly and honestly at your financial position and *then*:

- Reduce your expenditure if you are spending more money than you can afford to spend. Never mind if it hurts, do it.
- Deal with your debts by making *realistic* offers to your creditors to discharge the debts by a regular amount every month.

I have more to say about indebtedness in Chapter 4, but financial desperation is a disease that must be cured *now*, not later.

- Keep your creditors informed on an ongoing basis of your financial position so that they know that you are genuinely trying to meet your obligations.

- Keep things in perspective. Remember that, important as money, good financial management and solvency are for your general well-being and happiness, they are not the only things in life.

Of course, financial desperation is not the same as wanting to have more money than you have now. As we have seen and as we shall see, wanting to earn more money is a perfectly valid reason for setting up your own consultancy.

2

Planning your consultancy

Introduction

This chapter looks at how you should plan your consultancy, which means in broad terms planning which consultancy services you will offer and how you should start the process of setting up your consultancy.

I believe that the planning stage is essential to the success of your consultancy and that the specifics of forming your consultancy should only take place after you have carefully planned what you want to do.

Starting a high-income consultancy is in some respects an adventure and can be very exciting, but that does not give you an excuse to start behaving impulsively and erratically, any more than being impulsive and erratic will help you if you are involved in *any* adventure. Just as you will need to use your brain to its fullest extent when actually carrying out the work which your consultancy generates, you need to think hard at every stage of your consultancy's formation. Above all, you should hold in your mind a realistic assessment of your own strengths and weaknesses, and act so as to allow your strengths full play while concealing – and ideally also reducing – your weaknesses.

Why preparatory planning is so important

Starting a new consultancy, like starting any other new

business, is a profoundly creative enterprise, and like all truly creative enterprises, requires careful preliminary planning. Successful new consultancies do not suddenly spring fully formed into life, any more than successful novels, films or plays spring fully formed into life. New consultancies, like works of art, require planning and preparation.

So how do you plan your consultancy? The process is not as daunting as it may at first sound. What you have to do – assuming that you have decided that your life will not be complete unless you start your own consultancy (and ultimately if you do *not* feel this, you may not, after all, be sufficiently motivated) – is to first answer the fundamental question: *'What kind of consultancy service or services will I be offering?'* Then give some very serious and careful thought to answering the next question: *'What can I bring to this market as a consultant that existing consultants in this field are not already offering in a cost-effective way?'*

27

Let us look at these questions in detail.

WHAT KIND OF CONSULTANCY SERVICES WILL I BE OFFERING?

The answer to this question should arise naturally and easily out of your existing professional or vocational experience. The only situation in which you might need to give some protracted thought to what type of services you will be offering would be where you had detailed expertise in two or more areas, but were not sure in which area you should specialise.

For example, somebody with extensive experience in marketing may have to decide whether to set up as a marketing consultant, public relations consultant or advertising consultant. However, since it is likely that the two (or more) areas in which you have specialised to date will be related, it may be advisable for you to solve this problem by offering both types of service.

How extensive an experience of a particular specialisation is sufficient to give you the level of ability and knowledge which you will need in your life as a consultant? There cannot be a hard and fast rule about this; after all, people assimilate information at widely varying speeds, and what one person can master in a year, another person may need several years to absorb properly. However, I doubt very much whether you will have sufficient expertise and confidence to offer consultancy services in your specialisation, unless you have at least *five years* of experience in practising that specialisation. There may be exceptions to this rule, such as if you are one of the few people in your country who know about a particularly specialised field of expertise, but generally I think that the 'five year' rule holds.

Quite apart from the fact that you cannot expect clients to pay for your specialised and hard-won advice if your experience is *not* specialised and hard-won, it obviously makes sense for you to make as many business mistakes as you can at other people's expense: that is, *at the expense of the people who employ you during those five or more years*. There are quite enough mistakes which can be made *after* you set up your consultancy for you to have every reason to want to make fundamental business mistakes *while you are still an employee*.

Now onto the more difficult of the two questions.

WHAT CAN I BRING TO THIS MARKET AS A CONSULTANT THAT EXISTING CONSULTANTS IN THIS FIELD ARE NOT ALREADY OFFERING IN A COST-EFFECTIVE WAY?

Let me make this quite clear: you *must* have a good answer – and ideally several answers – to this question before taking the plunge and setting up your own consultancy. This is no time for dishonesty or self-delusion – indeed, when you are thinking of setting up a high-income consultancy there is *never* any time for dishonesty or self-delusion. You have simply got to ensure, before you take the plunge, that you can offer the market something which it does not, quite, already have.

What I mean here is that you need to find for yourself an

incremental advantage which will allow you to stand out from your rivals.

An incremental advantage

I mean by this the crucial, marginal competitive advantage which, in essence, is the idea which justifies the creation of your consultancy.

It will almost certainly have to be an incremental, marginal advantage that you are able to offer because unless you are exceptionally gifted, or very lucky, you will probably not be able to find an entirely new type of consultancy service to offer. On the other hand, there should be several types of incremental advantage which you can establish over your rivals.

I examine some of these types of incremental advantage in a moment. For the time being, keep firmly in your mind the unpleasant but incontestable fact that there are consultancies being set up in the business world all the time, and far too few of the consultants who run those consultancies have ever bothered to try to work out what they can offer that the competition cannot offer.

29

I am convinced that the principal reason why so many new consultancies do not survive more than a few weeks or months is that they have failed to identify the precise nature of the competitive advantages which they can offer.

What you really need to do here is to list your Unique Selling Propositions (USPs). This term, which I have borrowed from the world of marketing, refers to those special points which only you can offer and which will spur on clients to use your services, and nobody else's.

So what are the major types of incremental advantages or USPs? I suggest the following, but please do *not* regard this list as necessarily inclusive of all possibilities, because it is not. If you believe that you are able to establish a type of incremental advantage that I have not mentioned here, you may be right.

■ *A better knowledge of the market*

If you genuinely have a better knowledge of the market, or a better knowledge of a niche sector in the market, in which you are operating, you should be well on your way to establishing an important incremental advantage over your rivals.

Alex Dembitz, the Hungarian-born banker who heads the highly successful Geneva-based information technology IDOM Consultants, was able to get his consultancy off to a flying start by utilising his extensive knowledge of Hungarian business and the fact that Hungarian is his mother tongue. Alex was able to utilise this knowledge in order to sell his consultancy's rigorous and results-orientated information technology consultancy services to Hungarian banks who were keen to modify their operational structures and technological bases to make these suitable for trading within the market economies which prevailed in Hungary and other Eastern European countries after 1989. Alex obtained his first clients in Hungary, and having learnt exactly how he could help Hungarian banks to achieve what they wished to achieve, he took the logical step of developing his business to its utmost in Hungary while establishing offices in other Eastern European countries. IDOM now employs more than 170 consultants in Eastern Europe.

■ *An ability to provide less wordy reports*

Report writing – that is, making recommendations to your clients for action which you advise them to take – is an essential part of the consultancy business. The quality of writing which goes into many proposals which consultants provide to their clients is often very low. In particular, proposals are usually much too long. I do not know why this should be, but even highly experienced consultants all too frequently believe that it is better to use a long word in a report when a short one will do, and also that the more words you use the more profound or clever you are being. Both of those ideas are, of course, utter nonsense. William Shakespeare – the greatest writer of all – wrote 'Shall I compare thee to a summer's day?', not 'Would it be in my interests to effect a comparison between you and any unspecified twenty-four hour period that occurs at or around the summer solstice?' And what is good enough for Shakespeare should be good enough for you. The purpose of this book is not to teach you to write; you will have to go elsewhere for that; but all the same I strongly recommend that you follow these four rules when writing reports, assuming that you want the quality of your reports to give you an incremental advantage:

1 Never use a long word or phrase when a short one will do. 'Begin' is *always* better than 'commence', just as 'wordy nonsense' is always better than 'excessive verbosity that hinders the communications process.'

2 Remember, as Shakespeare had Polonius say in *Hamlet*, that 'brevity is the soul of wit'. In other words, the fewer words you can use to say what you want to say, the better.

3 Avoid repeating words on the same page if you can. The only exceptions to this are those short, familiar words like 'and', 'a,' 'the', 'is', 'are' and so on, which are the vertebrae of writing and which you can hardly avoid using fairly frequently. However, even with these you should try to avoid undue repetition if you can.

4 When you have finished the first draft of a report or indeed of any writing which you are doing for your business other than the shortest and most functional of letters, *always* get a print-out of the document and revise the print-out *before* inputting your revisions into the print-out to produce a final draft. I do not know why, but for some reason it is impossible to revise writing effectively when staring at it on a screen.

■ *A more cost-effective service*

Generally speaking, if you can undercut your rival consultancies on price and provide an equivalent or *ideally better* level of service, you should be able to get a foothold in whatever market you choose. Although there are always those clients who insist on believing that the more their consultants charge them, the better the consultant is, most clients have enough sense to realise that if they can get what they want from a consultant at a lower price, that consultant is worth using.

A moment's thought should show you that this particular possibility for incremental advantage should be very much in your favour as someone setting up a new independent consultancy. Whether or not you decide to begin by being a one-person band, or whether you decide to start your consultancy with one or more assistants or associates, you should have no difficulty in undercutting on price larger consultancies with higher overheads and more staff. I look at pricing in detail in the next chapter, but for the moment you should bear in mind that even in these relatively recessionary times (I am writing in August 1993) many large consultancies charge up to £2,500 *per day* for the services of a senior consultant, with junior consultants – who may only be a year or so out of college or university – being charged out at around £500 per day.

32

Of course, clients realise perfectly well that if they want to hire a consultant from one of the world's largest management consultancies they will need in effect to pay not only the consultant's salary but also a substantial contribution towards the consultancy's overheads, the salaries of administrative staff, and the firm's profit margin. However, the impression I have gained from observing the consultancy industry is that – whether as a result of the recession or simply because clients are fed up with receiving huge bills from large consultancies – clients are nowadays highly motivated to obtain their consultancy advice at a lower price if they can do so. *It is precisely for this reason that a chance of winning business exists for someone who is setting up a new consultancy from thin air.* As evidence of this, even large consultancies have had to look at ways of giving clients better value for money.

Incidentally, if you are planning on making price advantage one of your incremental advantages – and I suspect it is more than likely that you will be doing this – never describe yourself, whether face-to-face with a business prospect or in your corporate literature, as 'cheap'. Nobody wants to use a consultant who is cheap. I don't like the phrase 'competitively priced' either, because it is pompous and completely meaningless. Instead, say that you offer 'value for money', or are 'cost-effective'.

■ A more 'hands-on' service

This is an extremely important, yet not immediately obvious, way in which a new consultancy can make its mark. In the previous chapter I explained the need in today's consultancy industry for a consultancy not only to offer advice, but also to have the capability to put that advice into action. For a new consultancy, the ability to manage all the implementation necessary can be an important means of obtaining an incremental advantage. Obviously, the extent to which this applies will depend on the extent to which rival consultancies do *not* offer a fully hands-on service.

33

■ A more sincere, personal service

I have already emphasised that in the consultancy business it is ultimately personality that wins accounts. Even where clients are dealing with a consultancy which is large enough or which has been established for long enough to have acquired a corporate identity, clients will always regard themselves as dealing with a particular person or group of people at the organisation. The term 'a people business' is perhaps used rather too widely in the modern business world, but it is certainly true of the consultancy business.

I have no doubt at all that, as someone running a small or even one-person consultancy, you start with an inbuilt advantage in terms of giving your clients a sincere, personal service. When your clients deal with your consultancy they will be dealing with you, or perhaps you and one or two associates, but at any rate, you will be the lynchpin of the service that is offered to the client, and you can make that service personal and sincere.

Clients who deal with large consultancies, however, frequently complain that they have to deal with different consultants at different times. This, as can be imagined, is particularly a source of annoyance to clients who have found one consultant within the large consultancy who understands their needs and seems intelligent and helpful.

Another frequent complaint which clients level at large consultancies – not without justification, it has to be said – is that the team of people who win the business is rarely the same as the team of people who will handle the business. Most large consultancies have specialised 'new business' teams whose task it is to seek out and win new business for the consultancy and who often include, for obvious reasons, the most talented and dynamic people who work for the consultancy. Unfortunately for the client, in a large consultancy the new business team – which could be somewhat cynically regarded as a kind of bait – rarely actually works on the new business which it has won, with this business often being carried out by a lower calibre of person.

Clearly, for a start-up consultancy, the people who actually win the business will also be those who work on it. This makes for client goodwill, since the consultant will have been familiar with the client's business since the outset and will know exactly what the client is aiming to do.

Of course, this inherent advantage of the small, newly-founded consultancy will only apply if you can win enough trust and respect from your prospective clients to make them want to use your service in the first place.

■ *A more thoughtful service*

Small, independent consultancies are often able to offer a service which the client perceives as (and which may actually be) more thoughtful than that offered by rival consultancies, and particularly by larger rivals. The main reason for this is that the client is likely to perceive the small, independent consultancy as comprised of 'Chiefs' rather than 'Indians'.

Furthermore, a client will often be amenable to the idea that a small consultancy can provide a specialised service in a niche market, although if you want your client to believe this you will need to provide evidence of your abilities in the niche market in question.

I should hardly need to point out that even if the existing or prospective client does believe these things about your consultancy this will only be the case until you do something stupid which convinces the client that you are not that thoughtful after all. Don't give the client the opportunity to think anything other than that you and your associates are very exceptional and gifted people with whom the client should feel privileged to work.

■ A service which is backed by more specialised expertise

Closely related to the last point is the principle that a small, independent consultancy will usually be able to orientate itself around a niche specialisation (i.e. a specialisation 'within a specialisation'). As a rule, given that there is a demand for the niche specialisation; providing that niche specialisation – which is of course only possible if you have the requisite expertise – can provide an important competitive edge.

35

My own consultancy gains a competitive edge from occupying a niche specialisation. My consultancy is not only a public relations and editorial services consultancy, but a public relations consultancy that specialises in the high-tech and financial industries, as well as in the industry (the financial technology industry) which spans both these specialisations.

Alex Dembitz, who founded IDOM Consultants, found that his in-depth knowledge of the Western banking industry, coupled with the specialised knowledge of the Hungarian language and business scene gave him an unstoppable competitive advantage which allowed him – in the late-1980s – to become the leading Western consultant who was offering Western banking consultancy services to Hungarian banks. Of course, niche specialisations are only significant if there is a demand for them, but Alex had foreseen that there would be such a demand, and there was. Following his success in Hungary – which allowed Alex to recruit other consultants to work with him – IDOM expanded its activities to cover banks in other Eastern European countries: an interesting example of success in one niche specialisation leading to other niche specialisations, which in turn can cross national boundaries.

▪ A willingness on your part to take infinite pains

The famous writer and wit Oscar Wilde once wrote, 'talent is the capacity for taking infinite pains'. Being seen as someone who will stop at nothing to look after your clients is without doubt a way to establish an extremely important incremental competitive advantage. Ultimately, however, you will only be able to take infinite pains on your clients' behalf if you are truly devoted to your clients and if you love what you do. You can pretend for a while, but not for long.

36

Why you must get your first client before you set up your consultancy

Once you have worked out in what areas you are going to offer your expertise as a consultant, and you have got clear in your mind where you expect to score a competitive advantage over other consultants, your next job is to get your first client.

Yes, that's what I said: *your next job is to get your first client. That* is your first job, not forming your consultancy idea into a corporation, or obtaining office premises, or advertising for a secretarial assistant. No. Forget all those things. If you need to do them, you can do them – relatively speaking – in a flash. Your task, now, is to get your first client.

And if you think about it, what other way is there to start a new consultancy business *except* by obtaining your first client? What is a consultancy business, after all, but a way for one person or several people to help other people to run their businesses more effectively?

For goodness' sake don't get into your head the idea that a business is its premises, its logo, its stationery, and its bank account. It isn't. *A business is, and always has been, a relationship between a seller and a buyer.* It is true that when a business grows and develops, the nature of the relationship between seller and buyer becomes, to some extent, standardised – sometimes by the product that is sold being made into a 'branded' product – but the fact remains that what constitutes a business is the buyer and seller relationship at the heart of it.

This is true for all businesses, but as many businesses involve the buying and selling of a product, the relationship between seller and buyer becomes formalised, with the personalities of individual buyers often becoming unimportant. McDonald's would no doubt prefer it if you ate regularly at their restaurants, but if you personally decided tomorrow that you would never visit a McDonald's restaurant ever again, nobody at McDonald's would lose any sleep over it.

With a consultancy, however, one reverts back to the purest form of business: the personal relationship between seller and buyer. That being the case, isn't it slightly absurd to begin a consultancy without at least one such relationship to get you started?

By getting your first client before you start your consultancy in any formal sense you will gain the following benefits:

- Having got one client, you will have the confidence that you will be able to get additional clients.
- The nature of the service which you are providing to your first client will help to clarify in your mind precisely what kind of service you will need to offer as a consultant.
- You will have at least some income for the inevitably difficult first months when you have no salary payment coming in.
- You may, if you do a good job for your first client (as you must, if you want to survive) wind up with a client who is prepared to recommend you to other potential clients, or who at the very least should be prepared to give you a reference.

■ When you meet with prospective clients, it will be greatly to your favour if you are able to talk (in terms which, for reasons of client confidentiality, should be general rather than too specific) about a current assignment or current assignments on which you are working. Obviously you have got to start somewhere, and there will be that 'first client' who really is your first client, but it is never a good idea to let prospective clients suspect, even for an instant, that you are currently 'resting'. People think that an actor can 'rest' and still be good, but people do not look at consultants in the same way. Consultants without anything to do are regarded – not entirely unfairly, perhaps – as bad consultants.

There is, I am afraid, no easy answer to the question of how you get your first client. If you are the kind of person who – according to the five factors that I listed in Chapter 1 – has the aptitude to make a success of starting a new consultancy, and if you have completed the five years of minimum experience in your chosen field which I believe you need if you are going to consult for a living, you should already have numerous business contacts, any one of which may turn into your first client. You will need to bear in mind that if you are already working (or have been working) in a service business, you may need to abide by contractual arrangements that prevent you from working for one of your employer's existing clients for a certain period. Courts nowadays tend to take those contracts seriously, so you will have to be careful not to break the terms of your agreement, or not to break the terms openly. However, you are also likely to have potentially useful business contacts from jobs other than your current (or last) job.

With any luck at all you should be able to identify at least half a dozen business contacts who you believe could become your first client. Go and see all of them – in your own time, not in your current employer's time – and confide your plans to them. Even if they do not ultimately become your clients, they will appreciate your having confided in them and they may well help you out by telling *their* contacts about your plans, and about who you are.

38

In Chapter 6 I look at the all-important task of winning new business, but it needs to be said right now that *most consultants get the vast majority of their new business from personal recommendation, word-of-mouth and from existing clients*. There are other methods of obtaining new business, and these methods can be very useful, but ultimately personal recommendation and word-of-mouth are by far the most important ways to win business, whether you are starting out or after you have been a consultant for ten years.

Right, so now you have your first client, or even your first and second clients. Try to negotiate a deal with the client or clients which gives you, at the very least, enough money to meet your basic needs for six months, or a year if you can get it. This way, you will have some leeway while you work on the client's or clients' business and also build up your consultancy.

You've signed an agreement with your first client or first few clients? Congratulations. You are now ready to start looking at the specific practicalities of setting up your high-income consultancy.

3

Setting up your consultancy

Introducing the self-fuelling consultancy

I have named the type of consultancy which I describe how to set up in this book 'the self-fuelling consultancy'. This term is my own invention, and denotes a consultancy which is, from its earliest origins, 'self-fuelling', in that its growth and development are linked very closely to the demands of the marketplace rather than forced upon it, while the expenses of setting up and managing the consultancy should, with a very few exceptions, be funded by revenue that the self-fuelling consultancy is able to generate.

The self-fuelling consultancy is an efficient, streamlined consultancy which is geared above all to providing a first-rate service to its clients and to making the consultant or consultants who run it wealthy.

I was inspired to coin the term 'self-fuelling consultancy' by a writer whose book is the only other book – apart from Dale Carnegie's *How To Win Friends and Influence People*, of which more later – that I recommend to you as essential reading.

The book, *Growing a Business*, by Paul Hawken (Simon & Schuster, New York City, 1987) is the best business book I have ever read. Its quality stems both from Hawken's extremely lucid and clear style, and also from the sheer brilliance of his insights into the nature of business. Hawken uses the term the 'bootstrap business' to denote a business which starts small, grows organically, is funded substantially from revenue and seeks to win what Hawken calls the 'permission of the marketplace': that is, a genuine demand from the marketplace for the products or services that the business has on offer. In deference to Hawken's very considerable talents as a writer, I am not entirely happy with the term 'bootstrap business' for one reason and one reason only: due to Newton's law that to every action there is an equal and opposite reaction you will *never*, no matter how hard you try, manage to tug yourself off the ground by pulling at your bootstraps. For me, tugging yourself off the ground is a good metaphor for your consultancy taking off when you have devoted every atom of strength that you possess in order to make it succeed, so a bootstrap consultancy would be a little too earthbound for the purposes of this book. But read Hawken's book: it's a masterpiece of business writing.

In summary, the self-fuelling consultancy (I'll abbreviate this term to SFC for convenience) has the following key features:

- it starts small;

- its formation pares everything down to essentials;
- it does not involve you in risking a large amount of money in setting it up;
- it funds its growth as far as possible from revenue;
- it grows organically, in response to marketplace demand;
- it is run by people who are intelligent, committed, unpretentious and hard-working;
- it is fun to run and operate;
- it offers you real possibilities for earning a high income;
- it can be expanded to any size, given the proviso that the marketplace demand is there.

Can this be true? Is it really possible to set up a consultancy which requires minimal financial risk and which is fun to run and operate? Yes, such a consultancy is possible. The SFC is not a pipe dream but a reality. I believe that all successful consultancies once were – and many still are – SFCs.

Why you need to start small and grow organically

The first thing to remember, and the thing to keep in mind throughout all your time as a consultant is: *start your SFC on a small scale and let the size of your consultancy be dictated primarily by the amount of work that your clients give you, and only secondarily by your ambitions.*

On the face of it, this guideline is so obvious that there should hardly be any need to set it down. The trouble is that, however obvious the guideline is, most start-up consultancies fail to follow it.

Instead, what usually happens is that someone decides to set up a consultancy, whether alone or with various friends or business colleagues, and before you can say 'let's get into debt' the new consultancy has acquired an expensive office somewhere, expensive office equipment to fill it, a charming secretary, letterheads, compliment slips, company cars and the usual paraphernalia, and the consultant and his colleagues have given themselves important-sounding job titles and are raring to go.

Except that, because they have devoted their efforts to giving themselves the *illusion* of running a business rather than going out and getting clients, they don't have much to do. So they start bickering among themselves over whose job title is the most important and who is responsible for what. They finally agree on job titles and responsibilities, but there is still no work coming in, so maybe – if they have any money left – they employ a public relations consultant and/or advertising agency. By going down this route they are forgetting that public relations and advertising are all very well, but that these are essentially *additional* methods of obtaining clients, with the prime method of obtaining clients being the exploitation of one's existing contacts and/or clients, coupled with the widening relationship that goes with doing good work.

Not surprisingly, the new 'consultancy' finds that its efforts to

42

win business by using public relations and advertising don't work, but merely cost it more money. Perhaps, by this point, the consultancy *has* – through one consultant's contacts – been offered the opportunity to pitch for a potentially lucrative piece of business, but the consultancy's overheads are already so high, and the consultants themselves are getting increasingly desperate to start making some money, that the consultancy pitches its price for doing the piece of business at much the same level as the estimate provided by larger, longer-established consultancies.

As one might expect, the potential client can't see any reason to use the services of the new consultancy if the consultancy is not offering a cost-saving, and so the client gives its business to the larger, longer-established consultancy.

Result: morale at the new consultancy falls to an all-time low, and one of the consultants panics and takes a salaried job which has been offered to him by someone with whom he used to work.

43

Once this consultant has gone, the others, realising in their heart of hearts that he was probably right to leave, secretly start looking around for their own boltholes, then bicker even more intensely when these are not forthcoming.

Finally, six months or so after starting out, the secretary leaves when her last salary cheque bounces; the telephone service is cut off due to non-payment; the office equipment (most of which has been obtained on expensive leasing arrangements) is repossessed; and the landlord, whose rent has not been paid for two months, changes the locks on the doors and exercises his right to recover the premises.

The erstwhile consultants do their best to forget the experience and to return to the world of the regular salary, except that now they have all got embarrassing six-month holes in their c.v's, to say nothing of bank loans which must be repaid. This financial pressure makes it difficult for them to accept salaried jobs at a similar salary to what they were earning when they began their consultancy, and so they hold out for more lucrative positions, only to find that these are not forthcoming. Finally, they accept jobs at salaries which only just cover their living expenses and debt repayments. Their lives have taken a distinct turn for the worse, but sadly it does not occur to them for one moment to blame themselves for going about forming a new consultancy in a foolish way. Instead, they blame the recession, or what they regard as the pitiful lack of courage which their potential clients displayed in being unwilling to trust a new consultancy to do the job.

The above nightmarish scenario is not far-fetched, but is repeated again and again around the world, every week of every year. Indeed, if you think about it, where a new consultancy is being run by people who have allowed themselves to forget, even for a moment, *that a consultancy is only the sum of its relationships with its clients, and does not have any genuine existence apart from that*, it is difficult to see how the new consultancy can do anything *but* follow this rocky road to ruin.

Indeed, I have based the above scenario on two consultancies with which I have been personally involved: the first of which I helped to run when I was young and foolish and would have done a good deal better not to have believed that, with zero business experience, I could be a consultant; and the second of which I advised over its marketing at a time when the consultancy was, sadly, too far down the road to disaster for my advice to be of much avail.

As I observed above, the guideline that a new consultancy's size should be dictated by the amount of work which it has, is a pretty obvious kind of guideline, and in many ways can be reached by the simple application of commonsense. This being the case, why is this guideline so often implicitly disregarded by those who set up new consultancies?

I think there are two reasons for this, and both represent faulty business philosophy.

Firstly, many people who start consultancies believe that they will only be able to win business if they give their potential clients the impression that the consultancy is *already* well-established, with its own premises, staff, secretarial assistance and so on. There is only one problem with this idea: *it's rubbish.* The danger of believing that, as a new consultant, you need to expend a great deal of effort and money in order to give your new consultancy the pretence of being successful already (and of course it *will* only be a pretence) is so dangerous – so very dangerous – that it is essential for me to warn you very strongly indeed against it. *For goodness' sake don't follow that path; unless a miracle intervenes you will surely live to regret it.*

'But', you might say, 'If I don't give my potential clients the impression that my consultancy is already successful, how on earth can I expect to win any business from them?'

What a question. How can you ask it? Haven't you been listening? Go back to page 28 and read again what I said about the need for you to bring something to the market which existing consultants in your area are not already offering. Look again at the pages which follow, where I talk about the need for incremental advantage and show you the type of incremental advantages or Unique Selling Propositions which you might be able to display.

It is because of those incremental advantages that you can expect to win clients even though your consultancy is, in every sense, new and untested. Trying to convince your clients that you must have something to offer them because your consultancy *looks* as though it has been around a long time is not only deceitful and insincere (and you will perhaps remember that sincerity can in itself constitute an incremental advantage for a consultant) but it is also horribly expensive and may very likely turn out to be counter-productive because the effort of setting up a 'pretend' consultancy will probably blind you to the incremental advantages which you (and your colleagues, if you have any) *can* actually offer.

The second area where one often sees a faulty business philosophy at work is where people who have no experience of setting up their own commercial venture hold the naive and dangerous belief that setting up a new business is some sort of exciting game; and that renting premises, employing a secretarial assistant, buying word processors and telephone equipment, and getting your letterheads and compliment slips printed is somehow all part of that game. If you really believe this – and many people do – thank your lucky stars that I am around to advise you otherwise.

I'm not going to waste time on stating the obvious reasons why any idea that business is some sort of game is clearly nonsense. Just take it from me: *Business is not a game but a deadly serious battle in which there are no prisoners taken and in which everybody – both your clients and your suppliers – will be basically out to get from you whatever they can.*

I admit it: that is a slightly unnecessarily pessimistic view of what business is all about. Business *is* a battle, but it can be fun, too. There is no reason why, in the medium to long term, you should not be able to establish relationships with your clients and suppliers which are amicable, sincere, and mutually beneficial. *But*, and it is a big but, those relationships do not happen overnight, any more than the loving, mutually trusting relationship between a couple who have been happily together for several years can be compared with the relationship between a man and a woman who meet each other for the first time at a party and are not yet quite sure what they think of each other. Like the woman at the party (or indeed the man, for that matter) you would do well when setting up your new consultancy to cultivate a healthy *distrust* of the people you encounter while setting up your embryonic business, at least until you have good reason to trust them.

I can't help thinking that the media must shoulder part of the blame for giving people the idea that business is a sort of game where mere determination to succeed and the courage to set up in business by oneself are the qualities which will, by a sort of magic, bring you success and financial prosperity. I began my career in business in London during January 1984, when the boom of the mid-1980s was well underway and when, for perhaps the first time in history, the pride and excitement of setting up in business had become part of popular British culture. That this happened was in large part due to the gospel of enterprise and self-help which the ruling Conservative government under Margaret Thatcher had been preaching for several years. Newspapers and magazines were full of reports about people who were starting their own businesses; not necessarily *successful* businesses – since for the journalists who wrote these articles and the editors who commissioned them, what really mattered was that the person involved had the enterprise and guts to go it alone – but their *own* businesses, anyway.

Particularly popular were stories about management buy-outs (MBOs), or about people who had been made redundant from, or simply departed from, a traditional British heavy industry such as steel-making or mining and who had set up in business by themselves.

47

These stories clearly equated with the government's philosophy that Britain's future lay essentially in new types of business – particularly anything to do with high-tech – rather than in the traditional British industries which were no longer truly rarely competitive with overseas sources of supply.

I wonder how many of those new businesses that were applauded so loudly in the press in the mid-1980s are still flourishing today? Not many, I fancy. In retrospect, many of the new business ideas which received such lavish praise from politicians and the press alike during those days of the enterprise culture were slightly absurd. Businesses which involve fringe activities (as many of them did) such as going round offices in the City of London and selling luxury sandwiches are hardly substitutes for major national industrial infrastructures, laudable though the fringe business idea might be.

But the real point here is that, both in the mid-1980s and even in today's more recessionary and sober environment, press articles about people who start new businesses almost invariably tend to focus on the excitement and adventure of the enterprise, and hardly ever bother to stop a moment to wonder whether a real, lasting, market exists for the product or service being offered. Essentially, the message of these articles is that anyone can start their own business if they have the courage, enthusiasm and determination to make the business work.

Unfortunately, that isn't true. If there is no real demand for what a business is offering, then no amount of courage, enthusiasm and determination will make the business successful. Putting this idea in the terms of this book means facing the fact that unless it turns out that you *do* have genuine incremental advantages over other consultancies, your consultancy will not – indeed cannot – be a success.

And this is the kernel of the reason why you should and must start small, because *ultimately it is unlikely that you will be able to know with absolutely certainty whether you can establish a real and important incremental advantage until you have actually started working as a consultant.* Because you have wisely decided to follow my advice, you will not have started your consultancy at all unless you have one client onboard.

Very well, you have your client, and you are hoping very much that you will be able to get others, but you can't *know* for certain that you will be able to obtain other clients. So you start small, absolutely minimising the expense of your start-up, and you devote *every single atom of your energy as a consultant* to working hard for your first client or clients and looking for those other clients. You do not waste your energy in creating an artificial and pretentious corporate structure when you don't need such a structure. Instead you concentrate – concentrate utterly – on working for your existing client or clients, on searching for new business and on obtaining references from your satisfied clients; references which you can use in order to win more clients.

Follow that advice, and you will have the maximum possible chance of making your consultancy successful. Even if it turns out (and I'm afraid I cannot guarantee that it will not turn out) that you do not have sufficient incremental advantage firmly to

48

establish your consultancy as a source of high income for yourself (whether or not you decide to expand the consultancy) you will have risked a minimum of money on your venture. You will be able to return to the salaried world without any unpleasant debts hanging over you, and with whatever you did for your first client constituting a useful extension to your experience; and an extension of your experience which you can, with pride, include in your c.v.

Why you need to cultivate business sense before you begin

In the previous section I described the bad business philosophy which leads to the establishment of a consultancy that is not really a consultancy at all, but rather a pretend consultancy which is as lacking in real substance as a scarecrow. Being aware of the dangers of pursuing a bad business philosophy is extremely important for anybody who wants to start a high-income consultancy, but it would hardly be fair of me to introduce you to bad business philosophy without showing you what good business philosophy is all about. I now propose to do just that.

49

Good business philosophy – or 'business sense' as I prefer to term it here – is something with which some people are born but which most people have to learn, often through sad and costly personal experience.

In essence, business sense is the possession of a realistic awareness of how that part of human life which concerns itself with buying and selling really works, and a knowledge of how to get the best possible deal for yourself from the buying and selling world.

This awareness and knowledge is certainly not linked to your intellectual capacity. One of my favourite business stories concerns a fellow who was hopeless at arithmetic at school and who is still hopeless at arithmetic now but who, by virtue of his business sense, is a millionaire by the time he is thirty. One day he is visiting his local bar, where he bumps into a man – also now thirty years old – who at school had been top of the class at arithmetic every time. This chap is now an accountant, and makes a good living, but he is not a millionaire. The accountant bought the beers (the millionaire didn't mind letting him do that) and the two men chatted about their respective careers. 'I'm really pleased to hear that you've done so well,' the accountant says, after a while. 'Maybe there's something that you can teach me. What's the secret of your success?'

'Well', says the millionaire (please remember that he was hopeless at arithmetic), 'It's like this: I just happen to have this product which I buy for £5 and sell for £10. It's amazing how much money you can make on a 5 per cent mark-up.'

In his book *Growing a Business*, Paul Hawken uses the term 'tradeskill' to denote what I call business sense. This is what Hawken has to say (page 154) about tradeskill (the parentheses in the passage are his):

> Tradeskill is really the set of skills that spell the difference between success and failure in business. It is the knack of understanding what people want, how much they'll pay, and how they make their decision. It is knowing how to read the signals of the marketplace, how to learn from those signals, how to change your mind. Tradeskill gives you a canniness about how to approach a given product, market or niche. (The geniuses of tradeskill are the turnaround 'artists' who don't even need to 'know' the business they are in. They perform radical, successful surgery on the patient simply by knowing what the disease is.) Tradeskill becomes a sixth sense that gives those who have it the ability to make decisions quickly, cutting through months of meetings, brainstorming and bureaucratic shuffling. Tradeskill is knowing how to handle money, how to buy and how to sell.

In the film *Big*, starring Tom Hanks, Hanks plays a thirteen-year old boy who has grown into a man overnight as a result of making a wish at a mysterious magic puppet machine he discovered at a funfair. Hanks moves to New York City and finds himself a job as a lowly clerk at a corporation that designs and manufactures toys. He does not linger in his humble position for long, being promoted to the role of official toy-tester when his boss, played by Robert Loggia, notices that Hanks – who is at heart a child – possesses a remarkable ability for assessing whether or not a toy is likely to be successful in the marketplace. An extremely revealing sequence from the point of view of defining tradeskill occurs in the famous Fifth Avenue toyshop FAO Schwartz. Loggia and Hanks bump into each other there: Loggia having come to the shop to see what the competition is doing, while Hanks is there because he likes toyshops. During their conversation in the shop Loggia casually refers to a particular marketing report that he has been perusing, at which Hanks – whose character genuinely has no idea what a marketing report is – asks, 'What's a marketing report?'

Loggia takes the question as indicating that Hanks does not have a high opinion of marketing reports, and, giving Hanks a look that indicates a high respect for Hanks' perception, murmurs, 'Exactly'.

51

Possessing true business sense, as contrasted with the kind of dry, theoretical business lore which is taught by the vast majority of management books and most business courses, is the difference between how the characters played by Hanks and Loggia regarded the toyshop. Hanks walked around the shop with an instinctive feel for which toys were bad and which were good, whereas Loggia was all too aware of his own dependence on the purely cerebral, theoretical aspects of his business.

There is no reason why a highly intelligent and well-educated person should not also possess true business sense, but business sense is, in itself, anything but cerebral and theoretical. Rather, it is instinctive and is born out of a living, dynamic awareness of what business is and how business works. There are no substitutes for it.

In particular, pure theorising is no substitute for business sense because ultimately theorising merely forces a preconceived theory of behaviour on the dynamic elements – in particular market demand and how your clients view you – which will make or break your business. Business sense, on the other hand, apprises these dynamic elements in a holistic and genuine way, and draws realistic, instinctive conclusions about which course of action is likely to be in your best interests.

Having money is no substitute for business sense, either, although far too many people think that it is. In fact, as I go on to suggest in this book, possessing too much money when you are thinking of setting up your own consultancy is likely to prove a real handicap, not only because it may tempt you to make the fatal mistake of creating a 'pretend' consultancy which is not allowed to grow in organic harmony with the level of business that you can win, but also because the possession of too much money may blind you to the mistakes which you are making until it is too late to do much about them.

There is a very perceptive passage in Hawken's book *Growing a Business* (page 157), which neatly sums up what can happen when theory and money – rather than true business sense – are the bases for a new business. The passage relates to the retail industry, but the lessons which the passage has to teach us are profoundly important for anybody who is planning on setting up a new consultancy.

> Because California is immodestly affluent in some places, there are many businesses started up by professionals from other fields, including many couples who worked for large corporations and set out on their own. The results of these businesses, usually retail stores, are sometimes painful to watch. Because the owners are well educated, well connected and have 'good taste', they believe they have the advantage over other merchants. They don't – unless they have tradeskill. We have all seen the food 'shoppe' or toy boutique with the cute name, expensive custom-designed logo, well-chosen inventory, costly fixtures, beige carpet and articulate help. Nice touches, but why does the shop feel dead? We as customers sense a lack of hands-on knowledge, authenticity, and market sense. We want our businesses to be run by businesspeople, not by hobbyists. We're more comfortable in the hands of a pro than an amateur. Without tradeskill, a business seems a caricature of itself.

You cannot acquire business sense merely by following a set of rules, because there are no rules. Ultimately you cannot even know whether or not you possess business sense until you have gone out into the marketplace and made a success of running your own business – in this case your own consultancy. Unfortunately, it is possible to rise to a high corporate position – even, if the corporation is very well-established, the top position – without possessing much in the way of business sense. This can happen because a corporation is, in essence, somebody else's business; someone with true business sense has already been there and established the business before you joined it. When you work in a corporation which is already successful (which to some extent it presumably must be, or it would not be able to afford to employ you) the personal skills which are required ultimately boil down to conformity, restraint, getting on with the job and projecting oneself within a group of people. These qualities are all very well and good if you are content to remain an employee all your life, but they do not, of themselves, add up to the possession of business sense.

53

Sadly, many people think that they do, which is why every year millions of people throughout the world assume that since they have attained a high position in a corporation, they must be good at business. So they leave their nice, safe, salaried job behind and start their own business, only to discover – in many cases – that they can't make the business work. The reason they can't make the business work is that for all their achievements in their last corporate position, they don't actually possess business sense.

It would be absurd for me to suggest that *nobody* who has done well in a corporate environment is ever going to make a success of running their own consultancy, but I do want to drive home the point that your previous corporate experience will not *of itself* mean that you will be successful as an independent consultant. The skills which make a top-grade corporate executive are *not necessarily* those which will make you a good independent business person.

I know that earlier I stipulated five years of experience in the field in which you intend to consult as the minimum level of experience which you will need if you propose to consult independently, and I am perfectly aware that this experience can in most cases only realistically be gained within a corporate environment. However, there is no contradiction here, for I certainly have nothing against corporations. What I do object to – because it can be so very dangerous – is the assumption that success at a corporate level will easily lead on to success when running one's own consultancy. It might do, or it might not, but if it does that is because, in addition to your specialised knowledge of the areas in which you are consulting, you also possess business sense.

As I have said, there is really no way of telling whether or not you have business sense until you get to grips with the actual business of setting up and running your consultancy. All you can do, therefore, is follow my advice and keep your consultancy small at first, absolutely minimising your financial risk (more about that in Chapter 4) and only growing in response to the business that you are able to win.

Having said that, there is no reason at all why you should not set yourself specific *objectives* in terms of how much new business you are aiming to win in, say, your first year of trading and in successive years. I have objectives myself: I seek to win and work on as much profitable consultancy business as I can work on within my time constraints, which in my case include the necessity to spend time writing books to meet my commitments to publishers. You may well be devoting every single moment of your working time to consultancy activity, and as such you may want a more formal kind of objective; with, say, a specific target turnover being set for the end of the first year, and so on.

No, there is nothing wrong with objectives and targets, but I do not believe that setting them and thinking about them is a very useful activity, other than as something to spur you on when times are difficult. In any case, what objective does a consultant really need other than the objective of winning as much business as can reasonably be handled with existing resources and with resources that can be brought into play – even by subcontracting work to other consultants, if necessary – on the client's behalf?

Even so, I still maintain that you should start small and grow in response to market demand. That way, if you do discover that you are ultimately much happier working in a corporate environment, you can bail out in the manner that I suggested earlier, with whatever work you have done for your first client being a useful addition to your c.v. and with no nasty debts inhibiting your enjoyment of your return to the corporate fold.

Although I do not believe that anybody can teach you to have business sense, I do believe that there are certain fundamental business principles which, if you follow them, will give you at least the beginnings of business wisdom and may even prevent you from making many expensive mistakes. I have already touched on some of these principles earlier in this book, and I look at your approach to doing business in Chapter 5, but since it is now time to move on to the specifics of starting your own consultancy, you might find it useful for me to end this section by setting down what are, in my view, the 12 most important principles which will enable your consultancy to be guided by business sense.

55

1 Start your business enterprise small and only grow in response to your clients' needs, not in response to your own wishes and ambitions.
2 Never forget that business is a battle.
3 Take every possible step to minimise your financial risk.
4 Remember that only practical contact with your marketplace can tell you whether your business will succeed or not.
5 Always do a superb job for your clients and spare no effort to look after them.
6 Devote maximum time to working for your clients and winning new business, and minimum time to running your business. If you would like guidance on what proportion of time you ought to spend actively looking for new business (which includes attending new business meetings) rather

than working on existing client business, I recommend that you try not to spend more than one-quarter of the time looking for new business that you spend on working for existing clients. Of course, if, at an early stage of your SFC, clients are rather thin on the ground, you may want to spend proportionately more time on looking for new business, but when you start to get a good influx of work, I recommend that you go back to the 25 per cent rule.

7 Trust nobody – whether supplier, client or colleague – until they have proven themselves worthy of your trust.

8 Don't be afraid of admitting to yourself that you've made a mistake, but make sure that you learn from those mistakes.

9 Do not use the hours during which you should be running your consultancy to indulge personal fads such as hobbies and charity work.

10 Do not allow your consultancy to ruin your personal life. An unhappy consultant is rarely a good consultant.

11 Take every step to make yourself – and keep yourself – fit and healthy. If you do not already have a good doctor, get one.

12 Try to find a *mentor*: that is, someone against whom you can bounce ideas and with whom you can share your triumphs and disappointments over a beer or a glass of wine. A mentor should ideally be someone who is experienced in the business world, senior to you and for whom you have respect. There is no reason why it cannot be an uncle or aunt, or even your mother or father, if these people meet the qualifications. However, a mentor should not be someone who is actively involved with your consultancy, because such people will not be able to view your problems and queries with the dispassionate objectivity that is required. A mentor can be immensely beneficial for your morale, and can put your difficulties and tribulations in a perspective which will make it much easier for you to deal with them and, if things ever get really tough, survive them.

The 'thirteenth rule' here, by the way, is that you should not regard advice which others give you (including the advice in this book) as gospel until you have found it to work for you.

The practicalities of starting a self-fuelling consultancy

This final section looks at what you need to do in a practical sense in order to start your self-fuelling consultancy. I have broken down the process of starting your consultancy into six stages, with each stage being set down in sequence and individually discussed.

STAGE ONE: DECIDE WHETHER YOU WILL FORM YOUR CONSULTANCY ALONE OR WITH OTHERS

My advice on this subject is quite categorical: only form your consultancy with others if, and only if, you are unable to undertake the work which your first client or clients give you without the assistance of the others *and* if you have good reason to believe that you and your fellow consultants will be able to maintain this high level of business activity in the future.

Say, for example, your first client gives you a project which involves the need to visit 20 of the client's offices throughout the country and spend several days at each office gathering material for a lengthy, in-depth report which will make recommendations on how certain aspects of your client's business could be improved. Obviously you could not undertake such a large project yourself. On the other hand, it may be that this is the largest project which you can reasonably expect to obtain in your first year of trading. That being so, you would be very foolhardy to start your consultancy with two or three other people, merely because you were lucky enough to win such a big piece of business when starting out. You would do much better starting your consultancy by yourself, and hiring some other specialists on a temporary basis to help you out with this project.

If, on the other hand, the incremental advantage which your consultancy is able to offer is so good that you can reasonably expect to obtain large projects on a regular basis, you may want to consider forming your consultancy in conjunction with other specialists in your line of specialisation who are sympathetic to your plans and aims.

I say *you may want to consider* because, after all, there is no reason why, even if you do have good reason to believe that your consultancy is going to obtain major projects on a sustained basis, you need to start a consultancy in which you share your ownership of the consultancy with others. After all, that will dilute the equity in the consultancy, and if your consultancy is going to be a winner from the outset you may want to keep your hands on all the equity yourself, so that in ten years' time, when you are employing 100 people and are turning over £5 million annually, you have the option of selling your business and retiring to the Bahamas (except that any consultant who builds up a business in this way will be so much in love with his work that the last thing he will want to do is retire).

Given these factors above, why do so many new consultancies start out with four or five directors (each with their own painstakingly worked out job titles) and a secretarial assistant? The answer to this is very simple: the people who are founding the consultancy have no idea what they are doing. I cannot emphasise enough that trying to found some sort of 'ready-made consultancy' with several consultants and secretarial assistance is completely ridiculous if you do not have ample business to justify such a complex creation. And as I say, even if you did have enough business to justify this, you will probably do much better starting the consultancy on your own, and employing the other consultants.

Maybe you now want to protest, 'Oh, but I've worked with Rick, Dick and Mick for ten years and we've always had a dream of setting up a consultancy together.'

Sorry, but that isn't good enough. If you're thinking of creating a consultancy because you want to indulge in a dream, take my advice: keep your daytime job and have a week's holiday in Las Vegas to get all your desires for earthbound dreams out of your system. Starting a high-income consultancy is not about indulging dreams, it's about facing up to hard commercial realities about what the market is likely to want and whether or not you can provide it.

Having said that, don't let me put you off starting your consultancy with a few friends or colleagues if you already have some very interesting business in the bag and you are utterly convinced – and I mean *utterly convinced* – that you and your prospective co-founders are truly talented people who are sure to make a big success of setting up your consultancy together.

Otherwise, set up your consultancy by yourself. The road to the happy land of success in running a high-income consultancy passes through the valley of the shadow of anxiety, the sun-baked plains of hard work, the deep forests of confusion and self-doubt and the muddy trenches of inertia and exhaustion. Not only is it infinitely easier to give your consultancy the flexibility and adaptability it needs to negotiate these hazards if only one person (i.e. you) makes the decisions, but you will also want that promise of financial success to give you courage for the journey. On balance, the proper course to take is probably to start your consultancy by yourself.

Don't worry if you 'feel' that a business started by one person is not a 'real' business. Recognise this feeling as a leftover from the days when (probably) you worked in a corporate environment and were surrounded by people all day. Reflect that the average corporate person probably does only around three hours of real work a day, if you factor in coffee breaks, excursions out of the office, chats with colleagues about personal matters and the attendance at largely pointless 'internal meetings' where half a dozen people, earning together about a quarter of a million pounds a year, spend an hour deciding, for example, which brand of coffee machine ought to be purchased for the canteen on the second floor.

Resolve to work *solidly and with complete concentration* for at least six hours a day. That way, you will be doing the work of two corporate employees every day of your new-style, independent working life. Goodness me, your consultancy's already doubled in size, and you haven't even got it properly underway yet.

As regards how you organise the legal status of your new consultancy, I strongly advise you to start by forming your consultancy as a sole proprietorship, and only incorporate when (and if) you grow your business to employ at least four or five other staff, by which time the tax advantages of running a corporation, and the advantage which a corporation offers in most countries in terms of limiting your liability, will have started to become an important factor.

Otherwise, follow the basic rule of running an SFC, and keep the consultancy small; perhaps ideally a sole proprietorship. The precise benefits of starting your SFC as a sole proprietorship will depend on the laws of the country in which you are starting your SFC, but in general the main benefits of a sole proprietorship are as a follows:

- There is no legal requirement to file detailed accounts, although of course you will need to keep copies of your invoices and receipts so that you (or your accountant) can produce a truthful statement of your income during the year for income tax assessment.

- The costs of setting up a sole proprietorship are minimal, since in essence all you are doing is trading under a trading name.

- All income which your SFC generates can go straight into your pocket (given that you must, of course, keep records of your income for income tax assessment). With a corporation, on the other hand, you will need to invoice the corporation for your salary.

Against this, the sole proprietorship has the following possible disadvantages:

- Your liability is unlimited. For most consultancies this will not be a problem until they start to employ several people, at which point you will run into the problem that one of your staff might do something silly such as libel someone in a report they are writing or make a recommendation to a client which leads to the client suffering financial loss. For *some* consultancies, which specialise in areas (e.g. construction and engineering) where the possibility of being sued is a very real one, the sole proprietorship might not be suitable even when your consultancy consists of just you and (perhaps) a secretarial assistant.

You may want to take out professional liability insurance to prevent yourself suffering substantial financial loss if you are sued successfully, but such insurance is very expensive and not always available, and limiting your liability through incorporation will possibly be a better idea, given that you must obviously check the legal aspects of your incorporation to confirm that your liability is indeed limited. I look at insurance in detail in the next chapter, but it is worth mentioning at this juncture that professional indemnity insurance is almost always available more inexpensively through a professional institute than on the open market, so if you are a member of your respective professional institute, it is very much worth your while investigating whether your institute offers this insurance facility.

61

- As a sole proprietor, you will be taxed on the basis that the profit which you derive from your SFC is simply another element of your own personal income (which it is). In some cases you would pay less tax on your profits if you had incorporated than if you are a sole proprietor. However, whether this is true or not in your case is something that only your accountant can tell you, and any possible tax savings consequent upon incorporation must of course be set against the costs of setting up a corporation and the higher accountancy charges which go with that.

- Some business books try to persuade you that for a consultancy, the sole proprietorship is unprofessional and clients will prefer to work with consultancies which have incorporated. I do not believe this; it smacks of encouraging people to create 'pretend' consultancies, and you already know my views on those. The most profitable and most efficiently run consultancy for which I ever worked was run by a former journalist who had decided to offer public relations and editorial services (I later copied this idea when I began my own consultancy) and who traded as a sole proprietorship under a trading name, even though he employed several people.

If you are not offering consultancy services in an area where you consider that there *is* a high risk of being sued, I see no reason at all why the fact that you are not incorporated from the outset should prejudice your chances with prospective clients. It may be relevant to point out in this context that my own consultancy has been a sole proprietorship ever since I began to do business in 1988. I trade under the name 'James Essinger Associates', which appears at the top of my letterhead, with no 'Inc.' or 'Ltd.' following it.

The advantages and disadvantages of forming your SFC as a *corporation* can be summarised as follows:

Advantages of incorporation

- Limited liability.
- Possible savings on tax and National Insurance. These can be complex, and you need to talk to an accountant about them. For example, if your consultancy is really successful, there may be opportunities to receive part of your income in the form of company dividends, to which a lower tax rate and lower National Insurance may apply.

Disadvantages of incorporation

- Costs of incorporation.
- The expense of preparing detailed accounts to meet legal requirements.

- Income accruing to the corporation is not automatically yours.
- Lack of flexibility. For example, if you are a sole proprietorship and you want to change your trading name, all you need to do is change it. To change the name of a corporation, however, will involve you in expense.

The final option – inasmuch as anything which should be immediately disregarded *is* an option – is the partnership. The precise legal attributes of the partnership will depend on which country you are operating in, but, in general, partnerships involve joint and several unlimited liability, which is a nice way of saying that if you go into partnership with someone and that person screws up, you (and your other partners, if you have any) are as liable for the screw-up as is the person who made it.

In some professions, where the professional is not allowed to limit his liability, partnerships are the usual method of forming a firm. If, on the other hand, there is nothing to stop you from forming your SFC into either a sole proprietorship or a corporation, I advise you to forget about starting a partnership. Not only are partnerships inherently unstable, as partners are always falling out with each other and blaming each other for what is going wrong, but there are several complex legal niceties of forming a partnership, and the last thing which you want to be bothered with, when starting an SFC, are legal niceties.

Naming your self-fuelling consultancy

You need to choose a name for your SFC. In most cases, I recommend that you simply put the word 'Associates' after your name and leave it at that. But put 'Associates' rather than '& Associates' which is pretentious and outdated. If you are going into business with someone else and have decided to form the consultancy's name out of both your surnames plus the word 'Associates', the inevitable argument over whose name comes first will soon make you wish you had followed my advice and set up in business alone.

The rationale for basing your SFC's name around your own name is that what you are selling, as a consultant, is your own expertise and personality. And as I said earlier, ultimately it is personality that wins business for consultants. This being the case, it makes sense to be perfectly upfront and straightforward about the fact that, at least in the early days, it is essentially yourself and your experience and expertise that you have to offer. Besides, shouldn't what was good enough, among others, for Messrs Coopers & Lybrand, Messrs Touche and Ross, and Mr Arthur Andersen also be good enough for you?

I have always basically distrusted consultancy start-ups which call themselves silly things like 'Capable Consultants' or 'Consultancy Expertise'. There is a good deal of this silliness in the public relations industry, although I had better be careful about quoting hypothetical examples, since some of the real life examples are so silly that it might be that my hypothetical examples are already being used somewhere.

On the other hand, I have to admit that if your own name is either very boring or rather embarrassing, I don't *necessarily* advise you to set up your consultancy under that name. But if you need to pluck a name out of the air, choose a name which is straightforward and unpretentious. One good strategy is to choose a name which summarises what business you are in. For example, if you are an agricultural consultant and you do not want to include your own name in the name of your SFC, calling yourself 'Agricultural Consultants' is simple, unpretentious and effective, although you will have to check that nobody else is using the name.

STAGE TWO: DRAWING UP A BUSINESS PLAN

It is not at all clear that you need a detailed business plan to start a self-fuelling consultancy. You can, of course, draw up an imposing-looking document with lots of figures and financial projections, but even if you were to find such a document genuinely convincing (which I doubt) it is unlikely that professionals – and particularly your bank manager – would attach a similar level of credibility to it.

If you were planning to start a business which manufactured mousetraps, you would need to have some idea in advance of how many mousetraps you could expect to produce in your first year, how much wood and wire you would need to order and what you would need to pay for your materials, your machinery and your labour. Similarly, you would need to know how much you could charge for your mousetraps, and you would be well advised to plan for contingencies such as the Great Mouse Exodus to Hamelin taking place in your first year of trading.

But you are not starting a mousetrap factory; you are starting an SFC. And this being the case, I cannot see a business plan serving any function for you at all other than wasting time which would be better spent on clarifying in your head exactly what incremental advantage you can offer as a consultant, and on winning your first client.

65

If your answer to this is: 'Yes, but I need a detailed business plan so that I can apply to my bank manager to take out a loan to start the consultancy', then wait until the next chapter, where I show you how applying to your bank manager for a loan to start your new consultancy may not necessarily be a good idea.

In fact, as someone who is planning to start an SFC, the only business plan you really need is one which contains answers to the following five questions:

1 What consultancy services will your SFC offer?
2 What incremental advantages will you be offering your clients?
3 Who is your first client?
4 What will you be doing for them?
5 How will you set about getting your next clients?

You should already have answered the first four questions. The answer to the fifth question appears at various junctures in this book, and especially in Chapter 7.

Having said all this, there is probably something to be said for drawing up an informal business plan in which you set objectives and targets for, say, the first year of your SFC's operation. I never did this myself – I was too busy getting clients and looking after them – but I can readily imagine that many people might find the compilation of such a document highly motivating. I have already referred to the possible benefits of setting yourself objectives, and I would only add here that you must temper ambition and optimism with realism. There is not much point setting yourself objectives and targets which are so ambitious that a fair amount of success on your part leaves you feeling depressed because you haven't met your targets.

STAGE THREE: CHOOSING YOUR PREMISES

Knowing what you know by now about the SFC, it will not surprise you that I strongly recommend that you start your SFC at home.

The reasons for doing this are all very good reasons, and are as follows:

1 You need to pay your rent or mortgage anyway, so if you are working from home your premises will in effect not cost you anything extra.
2 You will probably be able to claim a proportion of your rent or mortgage as an allowable expense against income tax, although seek advice from an accountant here, since if you own your home it may be that making this claim may oblige you to pay tax on any profits you make when you eventually come to sell it.
3 Your office will probably be reasonably close to your bedroom, making it much easier for you to work long hours to deal with a heavy workload.
4 You will have no costs of travelling to work, and you will not waste time travelling to and from work.
5 Particularly in the early days, establishing a consultancy can be an anxious and lonely matter, and you will find it comforting to have your home comforts around you.

I had better mention the arguments which are usually raised *against* working from home. These arguments are:

1 *Working from home is unprofessional and ridiculous*

I don't hold with this argument. The entire principle of the SFC is that it is based around sincerity and good service. If you are (at least at first) a one-man band and are working from home, why pretend to be anything else? What matters to your clients is the quality of the service that you give them, not some spurious corporate framework that you have set up.

Unless you live in a complete slum, you can even have occasional meetings with your clients at your home. Clients who visit your house will probably appreciate the homeliness of the welcome that you can offer them. Besides, in these days of an unstable business environment, clients will have the confidence that they will know for the foreseeable future the whereabouts of someone who works from home, whereas someone who occupies a small rented office might vanish without trace.

67

2 *It is difficult to avoid being distracted when working at home*

I'm not convinced by this argument, either. If you can't concentrate on your SFC to the extent that you forget trivial domestic matters, I don't see how you are going to stay the course. In any case, working from home can actually help you to stop thinking about domestic anxieties. You won't need to worry about whether your house is being broken into, for one thing.

However, you *do* need a room which is entirely devoted to your SFC. When I began my consultancy in 1988 I lived in a house where I had to sleep and run my business in the same room. I wouldn't recommend that to anyone.

If you have a family, ask the rest of your family to respect the fact that your office *is* an office, not a playroom or a place to hang the washing.

If you are adamant about forming your SFC with other consultants and/or secretarial assistance, then find inexpensive premises which give you maximum flexibility in terms of terminating your rental agreement. Until you get a good idea of how exactly your business is likely to shape up, you will probably prefer to rent space in a self-contained business suite. Not only are these geared to the requirements of businesses which want to get into action quickly, but most suites have an in-house telephonist and secretarial facility which can be an excellent way of dealing with incoming phone calls and obtaining secretarial help without needing to employ a full-time person to carry out these tasks.

STAGE FOUR: CHOOSING YOUR EQUIPMENT

If you are initially going to be running your SFC as a one-man band, you will need the following office equipment, as a minimum. You can scale up this list to take into account what your colleagues will require.

Personal computer

I personally use an Amstrad PCW9512 dedicated word processor, but the nature of my business means that I spend much of my time writing, and this may not apply to you. I recommend that you use an IBM-compatible machine which has an accounting package and also a word processing package. Ideally everyone at your consultancy should have their own personal computer (you will probably want to network these computers in due course in order to share data and written material among all your colleagues and staff). Everybody should be competent enough at handling their computer to be able to produce professional-looking letters and reports without the necessary assistance of a secretary. Indeed, you probably will not need a full-time secretary at all, at least not in the beginning.

The reason for choosing an IBM-compatible personal computer

is that in due course you may want to supply documents to your clients in disc form, and the IBM-compatible format is the one which your clients are most likely to use. Before selecting your machines, get advice from a computer supplier over which disc size you ought to choose: generally speaking, the 5¼" format appears to be losing ground to the 3½" format, although both are still very much in use. Remember that your local computer shop ought to be able to convert files on one size of disc onto files on another size of disc if the need arises.

Telephone and fax

I recommend you start with a straightforward telephone and fax, keeping in mind the principle that you are going to be starting small and ought to minimise your outlay on equipment in the beginning. Combined telephone and fax machines are not a bad idea, except that they tend, by definition, to be rather large and may not always leave much room on your desk.

69

The basic problem with handling your fax arrangements is that fax machines which are supposed to be able to detect whether an incoming call is a fax or a voice transmission, and which are supposed only to activate if the incoming call is a fax, are in fact notoriously unreliable. If they don't work properly, anybody who makes a voice call to your office will hear only a fax tone, and this is incredibly irritating for the caller.

One way round this is to install a separate telephone line for your fax machine. This solves the problem, but additional telephone lines are expensive to install, and are sometimes not available to domestic residents.

Another way round the problem is not to bother buying a fax at all, but instead to make use of the services of a fax bureau to send and receive faxes. This solution is certainly workable, given that you have a fax bureau within reasonable walking distance of your office, but the big drawback here is that fax bureaus charge exorbitant sums for sending faxes, and you may find that after only a month or so of using your fax bureau you have already spent more money with them on sending faxes than you would have spent on a fax machine of your own. Fax bureaus also charge for *receiving* faxes.

So I do not recommend that you make abundant use of your local fax bureau for sending and receiving faxes. On the other hand, access to a fax is nowadays an essential tool for all consultants, so you really do need to be able to put a fax number on your letterhead which is not the same as your telephone number (unless you have a telephone/fax switching machine which is utterly reliable).

The two options which are open to you are therefore either to use an additional fax line or to install a fax in your office on your telephone line which you can use to send and receive faxes when you are in the office, and to use the services of a fax bureau for receiving faxes; putting the bureau's number on your letterhead.

Answering machine

There is definitely something to be said for having someone available to answer the telephone at all times. This is why, if you don't want to work from home, taking space in a business suite is a good move. In most cases the telephonist in a business suite will answer the telephone by saying the name of the suite and will then put the call through to your office if you are in, or else will tell the caller that you are not in and will request the caller to leave a message. Sometimes it is possible to arrange things in business suites so that you have your exclusive telephone number on the switchboard, so that when the telephonist sees that your number is ringing the telephonist can answer the telephone with the name of your firm.

Obviously, when you start to grow, you will probably have someone in the office all the time, anyway.

The only problem with incoming calls arises if you have decided to start your SFC at home. As I say, I strongly recommend this option if you are starting your consultancy by yourself, but I do concede that when a prospective client calls you it does not always create a very good impression if the client hears only an answering machine.

If you are working from home, there are three ways of resolving this problem.

Firstly, you can train your spouse (if you have one) to answer the telephone professionally on your behalf, although this does not, of course, cover the eventuality where your spouse is not at home. Note that on some occasions it can be efficient, from an income tax and National Insurance perspective, to pay your spouse a modest salary for doing this and other jobs for you. You will need to ask your accountant to clarify this.

Secondly, you can get yourself a mobile telephone, and include the mobile telephone number on the outgoing message that you leave on your answering machine. That way, people who want to talk to you when you are out can have the option of telephoning you on your mobile, assuming that you remember to take it with you.

71

Mobile telephones are no longer very expensive to buy, but making calls on them is extremely expensive. You should only use your mobile to initiate calls if the call is urgent and essential. Note that in some countries you also have to pay for calls which you receive on your mobile.

Thirdly, you can rely on your answering machine. If you choose this option, it is advisable to ensure that you are in the office on days when you are expecting more than the usual number of calls: such as the first or second day after you have sent out a mailing in search of new business.

Photocopier

I don't advise you to obtain your own photocopier until your business has grown to such a level that you absolutely need to have one in the office. Competition among photocopying bureaus keeps the prices of copying relatively low (this should also apply to the prices which fax bureaus charge, but doesn't seem to, presumably because there is less demand for fax services than for photocopying). Besides, photocopying anything other than a very short document is a horribly tedious task, and if you can get someone else to do it for you, at a modest cost, so much the better.

However, the principal reason for not having a photocopying machine in your office, unless absolutely essential, is that *photocopying machines are always breaking down.* I don't know exactly why this should be; presumably it is something to do with the delicacy of the mechanism which operates them. Whatever the reason, having a photocopier which constantly causes you stress and problems, and which necessitates frequent visits from a technician who will be quite happy to drink your tea and talk about football while he slowly gets round to fixing your machine, is hardly going to help you to run a successful SFC. Another, almost equally irritating problem with photocopiers is that they constantly seem to be running out of that black powder which they use to create the image on the paper. Oh, and the paper itself gets stuck inside much of the time, too.

Bearing all this in mind, it is much better to let a bureau do your copying and for you to get on with more important things.

Furniture

Office furniture – which I take mainly to include desks, chairs, filing cabinets, bookshelves, bookcases and waste paper baskets – is something which you should try to obtain as inexpensively as possible when starting your SFC. The only exception to this rule concerns your office chair or chairs. I firmly believe that the comfort of the chairs in an office is a major factor in the morale of the people who work in that office (even if 'the people who work in that office' only means one person i.e. yourself). It never fails to astonish me that many people who work in offices are prepared to sit on those dreadful little metal chairs with short backs shaped like the end of a canoe paddle. Since you will be spending many hours sitting on your office chair, the least you can do is make yourself comfortable, which means that you need a chair with a high back for the best level of back support and ideally also with side supports so that you have somewhere to rest your elbows while you are typing on your computer keyboard.

Bad backs and even more serious problems such as repetitive strain injury (RSI) are very common among office workers, and I am convinced that much of the problem stems from sitting for long periods on an uncomfortable or unsuitable chair.

One final point about office equipment: *never buy any piece of office equipment on a leasing arrangement.*

The money you will save by following this particular piece of advice should itself outweigh the cost of this book several times over.

Leasing arrangements are just about the nearest thing which there is in the business world to daylight robbery. What happens in a leasing arrangement is basically this: you sign an agreement, make a relatively low initial payment and obtain a certain piece of equipment. That sounds easy, doesn't it? Except that the agreement condemns you to pay a regular sum to the leasing company over a period of years, at the end of which (assuming you survive the experience) you have not only paid the retail cost of the equipment several times over, but – to add insult to injury – you will also receive a letter from the leasing company asking you to return the equipment to them or otherwise pay a final termination fee. If you do pay this final fee the equipment is still not legally yours, but remains the property of the company forever; meaning that if you ever want to get rid of it you're not even allowed to sell it, but must return it to the leasing company. Believe it or not, some leasing companies actually telephone their ex-lessees from time to time to check that the lessee has not sold the equipment.

Some leasing companies supply photocopiers on quasi-leasing arrangements where you get the copier installed ostensibly

73

'free of charge', then pay for the number of copies that you make. These agreements are absolutely lethal, for in most cases you get charged for a minimum number of copies every month whether or not you actually make that number of copies, and I hardly need add that the agreement which you sign at the beginning commits you to paying this regular sum until it is just about time for you to retire.

Now, of course, leasing companies know that nobody in their right mind would sign agreements like this unless there was a big carrot attached to the stick. What they like to do, therefore, is to sell their leasing arrangements through small, friendly, local vendors (that nice old chap who runs that little shop down the road, for example). These vendors are offered inflated commission rates in return for persuading idiots to sign up. Of course, even though you might sign the leasing agreement in dear old Fred Bloggs' office while he tells you about the holiday he had last month in Connecticut or Cornwall, the organisation with whom you are signing the deal is actually Bloodsucking Leasing Incorporated, and once you've signed, you're lost. You'll probably only have signed in the first place because Fred has successfully persuaded you that the deal involves him giving you a replacement piece of equipment every year while the agreement is in force, and of course you get something such as a free alarm clock from Fred as another reward for having signed yourself up.

All well and good, until you read in your local paper the following month that Fred has gone out of business. By this time the alarm clock will have irretrievably broken down, so you contact Bloodsucking Leasing Incorporated to find out where you stand in relation to getting your equipment changed every year, only to discover that of course that won't be happening now, as Fred has ceased trading, but that the agreement which you signed naturally remains in force. And believe me, if you thought Perry Mason was an efficient lawyer, wait until you see the debt collection departments of leasing companies spring into action.

The moral of this is: tell any leasing companies or their agents who approach you to stuff their leasing agreements where the sun never shines. If you really cannot afford to pay cash for a piece of equipment that you need, consider taking out a bank loan to do so; the interest rate will probably be lower than that 'offered' by leasing companies and you will not be tied to some extortionate agreement.

STAGE FIVE: FILING

I firmly believe that the key to the effective and rapid administration of an SFC – indeed of any business – is the maintenance of a good filing system.

The key to a good filing system is twofold: simplicity and an awareness that the best filing cabinet of all is your waste paper basket.

Above all, keep your filing system simple and up to date. Use jacket files to keep all relevant papers relating to the current work you are undertaking for each of your individual clients, and use a different coloured file for each client so that you can easily distinguish between files. *Keep your clients' 'current files' close to hand, so that you can easily grab the file when a client calls without having the client hanging on the telephone for five minutes while you search for the file.* For some clients you will also need back-up files to keep background information which is not needed for the current project or projects but which ought to be accessible.

75

Keep another file containing copies of all invoices that you have issued, and wait until your clients have paid the invoices before putting the invoices into yet another file, which should hold all the receipts, copies of paid invoices, and other items which your accountant will need.

Put receipts into that file as and when you obtain them. Remember that you will usually need to show receipts for any legitimate business expenses in order to offset them against tax, so try to obtain receipts for all expenses. If, say, you are planning on claiming for a regular small cash expenditure, such as the daily copy of the *Wall Street Journal* or the *Financial Times* which you buy from your local newsagent, he will probably be prepared to give you a receipt for these on a weekly basis, even if he would not be happy about you asking for a receipt every time you made the purchase.

You will also need a separate file for client agreements, unless you prefer to put these into the respective client files. However, it is probably best to keep these very important documents separate from the files in which you are keeping records of day-to-day client activity.

Keep a 'day file' where you can keep all letters which you receive through the mail and which are significant for your business. You can also put into your day file copies of important letters that you *send*. Day files need sifting through every month or so in order to remove items which you no longer need.

76

You will also require an efficient method of keeping names, addresses and telephone numbers of contacts, as well as the business cards which you are given and which you want to keep. A rotating business card file – which allows you to store the cards in alphabetical order – can be very useful here, although it doesn't solve the problem of what to do about those contact details which you want to jot down yourself and retain. I myself prefer to use a notebook with an alphabetical index, into which I paste important business cards and also write down key contact details. However, the method that you use here is obviously a matter of individual taste.

When it comes to filing, there are three rules which you ought to keep in mind.

First, there is the golden rule of filing: *when you have anything to file, file it immediately*. This particularly applies to your incoming mail. When you have sifted through your mail and binned what needs binning, it is very tempting to put the remaining mail in a little pile somewhere in your office and get on with whatever job you are currently working on. Don't do this. Instead, get into the habit of filing your incoming mail immediately into the relevant files.

The silver rule of filing is: *always be alive to the dangers of filing something in the wrong place.* Analytical scientists would tell us that paper is a lifeless substance; a mere wood product which, by the time it reaches us, has been pulped, pulverised and bleached to the extent that what remains bears no resemblance whatsoever to a living tree.

Don't you believe it. In fact, paper has a life of its own, and it is a strange facet of running a business that the more critical and crucial a particular letter or document is, the more likely it is to attach itself by a sort of magic to the underside of a sheet that is ready for the bin, or the more probable it is that the prized piece of paper in question will manage to get itself filed with a routine document that you bury in one of your other files. Then, when you are sifting through the file a month or so later, you find the document whose apparent loss caused you so much heartache and inconvenience.

77

The only way to prevent this problem is to take great care with documentation and to concentrate when you are handling it, rather than imagine that documentation is something which is so easy to handle that you can easily file it away with one hand while you are holding the telephone receiver in the other hand and engaging in an important telephone call.

The bronze rule of filing is: *don't be afraid to use the waste paper basket as an important part of your filing system.* Generally speaking, most businesses retain far too much documentation on file. This is all very well if the business is a long-established organisation where keeping on file a letter which Mr Fox wrote to Mr Rabbit in 1923 is a way for the organisation to remind itself of its traditional origins. However, you are starting an SFC, and the more streamlined you are, the better.

Of course you have to hang onto documents for several years where there is a legal requirement to do so (this applies to your financial records used for accounting purposes, for example). But apart from that, it is usually better to bin papers which are no longer part of your current activity. I would generally say that you ought not to bother retaining any paper or documentation *that is no longer being actively used* for longer than six months unless there is very good reason to do so. On the other hand, if you would feel much safer keeping every single document that passes through your office, don't let me stop you.

STAGE SIX: CHOOSING YOUR STATIONERY

As you should by now be very much aware, I believe passionately in the need to start an SFC small, run it as cost-effectively as possible and to take every step to relate its growth strictly to the volume of business that you generate for your SFC. However, while starting small and running your SFC cost-effectively will mean that you need to cut corners with some expenditure *you must make every effort to furnish yourself with professional-looking and attractive stationery*.

78

The reason for this is simple: your stationery is the way in which you present yourself to the business world through the mail. If you are offering an intelligent, thoughtful and resourceful service, it will not matter that you are working from home and (for the moment) only paying yourself a minimal salary. Nor does it matter, really, that when you are not in the office your prospective clients will (for the time being) have no alternative but to leave a message for you on your answering machine. You are just starting out; and by keeping things simple and even slightly primitive you are minimising your expenditure and ensuring that you focus all your efforts and energies on working for your first client or clients and on searching for new business.

But you cannot economise on stationery. If you do, your clients will (with reason) regard you as being amateurish and even slightly crazy.

I am not suggesting that you need to spend thousands of pounds doing what large corporations do, and getting some hyped corporate image firm to design them an entirely new corporate image, with a custom-designed typeface. On the other hand, if you seriously think that it is in the best interests of your SFC for you to write letters to your prospective clients which are merely typed onto plain paper, you are wrong.

What I recommend is that you go to a local commercial designer and ask him to provide you with samples of typefaces suitable for stationery, given that you will probably need one typeface for the relatively large letters which present the name of your SFC, and another typeface for the smaller letters and numbers which present other information. You can also ask the designer for some suggestions regarding the colour of the letters and numbers on your stationery. Keep this to just one colour in order to minimise printing costs. I have always found that dark blue is a strong, attractive, business-like colour, but you may have other ideas.

Some franchised chains of printing shops offer special deals on stationery design and printing to new businesses. If you shop around you will probably find that you can get your stationery designed and the first batch of it printed at a very reasonable cost.

79

As far as what specific stationery you ought to order; you will, as a minimum, need to equip yourself with the following.

Letterheads

These are the flagship documents on which you present your SFC through the mail. The letterhead is the piece of stationery on which the first page of your letters appears. It must contain the following information:

- the name of your SFC;
- the address of your SFC;
- the telephone number, fax number and (if you have them) telex number and mobile telephone number of your SFC. Remember, incidentally, that if you have a serious expectation of being able to win business from abroad, a pleasant courtesy to your prospective foreign clients is to put your own country's national dialling code on the letterhead.

You can put other information on your letterhead, such as the names of your fellow consultants, if you have any, or simply your own name and job title. It often looks better if the name or names of personnel are at the foot of the letterhead rather than at the top.

By the way, if you are running your SFC alone, want to put your name on your letterhead and don't know how to describe yourself, call yourself 'managing consultant'. This is simple, unpretentious and – best of all – true.

Some consultants like to put relevant tax numbers and any incorporation numbers on their letterhead. Whether or not you do this is a matter of taste.

Continuation sheets

80

These are the sheets of paper on which you type (ideally with a word processor) your letters and other documents after the first page, which will go on your letterhead.

Many consultants do without continuation sheets, preferring instead simply to use a sheet of plain paper. However, I recommend that you do obtain continuation sheets, for two reasons.

Firstly, they make your letters and documents look very professional.

Secondly, it is very likely that the type of paper (which is determined by factors such as the weight of the paper and the watermark on it) which has been used for your letterheads will not be the same as your everyday plain paper. If you do not use a continuation sheet, you may find that there is a very unprofessional-looking contrast between the appearance of your letterhead and the appearance of your successive sheets. Of course, if you do decide to use continuation sheets, make sure that the type of paper on which they are printed is the same as that which has been used for the letterheads.

Your continuation sheets should simply carry, in the top right-hand corner, the name of your SFC as it appears on your letterhead, but the name should be reduced in size by at least one-half for the continuation sheets. This is simply because it makes for a neater and more professional appearance than if your SFC's name is reproduced on the continuation sheet the same size as it appears on the letterhead.

Compliment slips

You should include a compliment slip whenever you send somebody something (e.g. an invoice or a cheque) that doesn't require an accompanying letter. They should contain the name of your firm, and all the contact details, plus the words 'With Compliments'. I always think that the words 'With Compliments' look better when printed in some mock-archaic typeface, but that is only my opinion.

Invoices

Now we come to the mighty invoice, the life-blood of any business, and the one thing which you will never regret giving away.

An invoice is usually a one-page document – the same size as your letterhead – with one or more copy sheets underneath. You send the top copy to the lucky recipient, and you keep the bottom copy or copies for your files in order that you know what invoices you have issued and can keep a track of those which are still outstanding, and also so that you can keep a record of your SFC's revenue.

There are many ways of composing invoices and it would not be appropriate for me to urge you to compose invoices in a particular way, except to say that if you are imposing a statutory tax on the amount invoiced (e.g. value added tax in the United Kingdom) you should put your registration number for this tax on your invoice (in some countries you are legally obliged to do so).

As a minimum, your invoices ought to contain the following information:

- the name of your SFC and your contact details. These are normally placed at the top of the invoice, and there is no reason at all why they cannot simply be 'lifted' from your letterhead;

- a space for you to write or typewrite the number of the invoice (incidentally, when you do get round to issuing your first invoices, don't make yourself look silly by starting with invoice numbers 1, 2, 3 etc. but instead start with 101, 102, 103 and so on. This isn't insincere or dishonest, but simply the application of business sense);

- a space for you to write or typewrite the date of the invoice;

- a space for you to write or typewrite your customer's name and address;

- a space (which should be the largest space on the invoice) for you to write or typewrite details of the activity which you have performed (or are performing or are about to perform) and which is the reason for sending the invoice. Remember, by the way, when you do get round to sending invoices, to distinguish clearly on the invoice between consultancy time for which a fee is payable and agreed expenses;

- a column in which you write or typewrite the various sums of money involved. If you are charging a statutory tax in addition to your own charges you will need to create an extra little box for this, and a box for a sub-total prior to setting down the total;

- you might like to state your payment terms at the foot of the invoice. But if you do this, don't make your words sound dictatorial. At the foot of my invoices I put 'Payment Within Thirty Days Would Be Appreciated'. I find that this gets things moving without annoying clients.

Business cards

These are essential. As with your other stationery, they should conform to whatever typeface and colour scheme you have chosen. I recommend that you keep what appears on your business cards simple and functional. You will need to put the name of your SFC and your contact details on the card, so I suggest that again, you simply lift these from your letterhead. Apart from those details, you also obviously need to put your name and job title on the card, not forgetting to include any letters after your name. Legitimate letters to include after your name would be those accruing from a first and second degree or a doctorate, as well as any letters which you have by virtue of belonging to a professional institution *which allows you to use those letters*. Do not use letters after your name which you have concocted; somebody is bound to find you out sooner or later.

That, then, is an overview of your minimum stationery requirements. The other item of stationery, which you *may* need, is a brochure or leaflet which gives details of the services which you offer to prospective clients.

I was in business successfully for two years before I bothered to produce such a brochure, and I have never really found that new business mailings are any more or less successful when I include a brochure in the mailing with the letter, as I believe it is the letter which really matters. There is also the point that brochures tend to date easily. This may be because you have acquired some new clients who take your SFC in a slightly, but significantly, different direction to where you thought it was going, or because you have decided to include, with their permission (make sure you get this) the names of your clients in your brochure and you then find that some of these clients stop being clients, while other clients come onstream.

83

Generally speaking, I strongly recommend that you do *not* produce a brochure until you have been trading for at least six months, after which period you will be in a better position to assess what exactly you ought to say in your brochure. If the basic business idea (i.e. the incremental advantage or advantages) behind your SFC is any good, you should have no problem in trading successfully for those six months, after which time you may find yourself so busy that you will not want to bother with a brochure after all.

If you *do* produce a brochure, don't spend too much money on it and avoid using pompous and boastful language about what your SFC can do for its clients and what your own skills and expertise are. Keep what you say factual and to the point. I'm not going to write your brochure for you, but you may find the following headings useful when deciding on its structure. I suggest that you divide the brochure into various sections, as follows, with the order in which I present them here being one possible order in which they could appear in your brochure:

1 The name of your firm and its contact details.
2 A one-sentence summary of what your SFC has to offer.
3 An explanation of what your SFC is and who is or are working for it.
4 A detailed but concise account of what your SFC offers its clients.
5 Details of why you regard your service to be cost-effective, and concise information about your charges.
6 Examples of your clients. You must get permission from your clients to include their names here, and if you don't have at least six clients to put in here, don't have this section at all. Instead, say something vague like 'references are available'.
7 Flattering comments – such as extracts from letters – which your clients have directed at you. But do make sure that the client doesn't object to your using these comments in your brochure. You should also say somewhere in the brochure that references are available from existing clients if required, and then if someone pursues this, you can put them in touch with the client who you know most likes you and admires you.
8 The name of the person at your SFC who clients should contact, and that person's telephone number (repeated).

STAGE SEVEN: LOOKING THE PART

I propose to keep my comments on this stage short and to the point, which does not mean that I do not regard this stage as being of enormous importance, because I do.

The lesson here is simple: *if you are going to be a successful*

84

consultant you have to look the part from the outset and never stop looking the part.

I am not talking about what you look like when you are working in your office. Of course, if you are working in your office with colleagues you should look fairly smart in order to ensure that there is a general air of professionalism in your office. However, if you are working alone what really matters is that you are able to work with maximum efficiency and energy, and if that means that you don't shave (assuming you are a man) all day and work in your pyjamas (or nightdress) until noon, that's fine by me, except that I really think you'd feel more professional talking on the telephone to the head of a billion-dollar corporation if you weren't wearing your pyjamas.

What I am really concerned about here is that you look great when you attend meetings. Smart business clothing is so much a part of success in business – especially for women – that it really ought to be a tax-deductible expense. Sadly, it isn't.

85

However, this point has at least given me an easy link into the next chapter, which is all about money.

4

Money

Western attitudes towards money

The Western world has always held a hypocritical and paranoid attitude towards money. While, on the face of it, the values which underlie life in the West stem from such aspects of traditional morality as the importance of the family, the work ethic and the basic tenets of Christianity (even though Western societies are now essentially secular societies), what really underlies Western society is an immensely high regard for the importance of money and an almost obsessive awareness of what the possession of money means for the individual.

I am not making a political point here; merely suggesting that the attitude which Western society holds towards money is, to put it mildly, confused.

Furthermore, in most Western societies money is supposed to be something which respectable people obtain by a kind of osmosis; with money flowing into them through their skins without them actually having to do any work in order to obtain it. Money is supposed to be something which people are expected to have – with poverty and insolvency being regarded as things to be terribly ashamed of – but people who talk about money all the time and who are seen too obviously to be doing their utmost to make money are regarded as both coarse and slightly untrustworthy.

What does this mean for you as someone who is starting a self-fuelling consultancy? What it means is that you have to face the fact that you are living in a society where the *principal aim* of your SFC – the acquisition of money – is theoretically frowned upon by society at large, and therefore also by your clients, who will not have any objection (assuming they are honest people) to pay you what you have legitimately earned by working for them, but who will not want to see you making money too *overtly*.

As a consequence of all this, in your financial dealings with your clients you must be careful to bear in mind the following:

1 You must never behave in such a way as to let your clients see that you are financially desperate.
2 You must never come over to your clients as being financially greedy.
3 No matter how eager you are to earn money, you must always ensure that your clients regard you as someone who is, above all, concerned with doing a *good job* rather than with the financial reward which will follow the completion of that job.

87

In other words, your own attitude towards money must become slightly hypocritical, with you giving the impression to your clients that basically you work as a consultant because you love your specialisation, and that the money itself is not really that important to you.

This *is* a hypocritical attitude, because the truth is that *you cannot possibly expect your consultancy to succeed at all, much less to become a high-income consultancy, unless the financial side of your SFC is, from the outset, a major preoccupation of yours, and remains a continuing preoccupation, whatever size your SFC is destined to reach.*

Why you must be preoccupied with money

When starting and running an SFC, you have no choice but to be preoccupied with money. *Money is: (a) the life-blood of your SFC; (b) a key motive for starting and running it; (c) a measure of how well you are doing; (d) the most important result of your success.*

It is not the *only* result of your success, but it is easily the most important one. The enjoyment of being independent and your own boss, and the pleasure which you obtain from practising whatever professional specialisation is behind the foundation of your consultancy, will also be important results of your success. Money, however, is more important than these, for if your SFC does not succeed financially then you will not enjoy being independent, or practising your specialisation, for very long, as financial problems will upset you and will ultimately force you out of business.

So let me emphasise this fundamental point again: *if you want to make your SFC a success you have no alternative but to be preoccupied with money all the time that you are running your SFC.*

88

Which means that, even if you personally are the sort of person for whom what really matters in life are things that are not essentially money-orientated, whenever you are fulfilling the role of running your SFC you must force to the front of your mind the belief that the acquisition and retention of money *is* the most important thing in your life. In my own case, the most important things in my life are, in order of importance: love, literature, friendship and the countryside. However, I never allow myself to forget that without money, none of these four great enjoyments are accessible. (Yes, I know that there are some idealists who would say that having access to love and friendship are nothing to do with the possession of money, but I am not such an idealist.)

If you do *not* run your consultancy as though the acquisition and retention of money were the most important thing in your life, you are almost certainly heading for disaster. You are heading for disaster, because you will either spend too much money on operating your consultancy, or you will get into debt, or you will not make enough money from your business, and any one of these problems (although they have a horrible tendency to come along all together) will land you in financial hell.

Financial hell

Financial hell is a terrible, terrible place, and you must avoid it at – literally – all costs. Financial hell means being in debt and not being able easily to clear your debts. It means not earning anything like enough money from your consultancy to pay your living expenses. It means getting official demands for income tax and other statutory taxes, and being unable to pay them. It means going to bed worrying about money, getting up worrying about money, and spending the day worrying about money. It means that when you have breakfast with your spouse, and they are bright and cheerful, you regard their brightness and cheerfulness not as something to be delighted with, but rather as displaying an insulting level of insensitivity to your own feelings. It means not being able to give your children the treats and pleasures that you would like to give them. It means being terrified to open the morning's post, for fear of what you might find.

It means that everything in your life, everything which you value and love, is tainted and even ruined by your financial anxieties. It means, no doubt about it, being in hell.

And the sad fact is that every year, of all the numerous people throughout the world who set up as consultants, a horribly large number of them wind up in financial hell.

Say to yourself: *I am not going to be like them.*

Say to yourself: *I am starting my own consultancy in order to make more money than I have ever made before in my entire life. I am starting my own consultancy in order to liberate my spirit from the tedium and humiliation of being a salaried employee, and in order to practise a specialisation that really interests me. I am not starting my own consultancy in order to enter financial hell.*

That last point is something you must never forget. Say it again: *I am not starting my own consultancy in order to enter financial hell.*

Unfortunately, merely resolving that you are not starting your own consultancy in order to enter financial hell will not stop you entering that hell, any more than if you jump off the top of the Empire State Building, resolving on the way down that you are not going to die will help you to avoid that fate.

And make no mistake about it: *entering financial hell is dreadfully easy.* And once you have entered it, emerging from it, while possible, is very difficult. For financial hell is in many ways like those 'black holes' which theoretical physicists tell us are formed in outer space when a star collapses, creating such a prodigious mass and such a massive consequent gravitational attraction that everything, even light itself, is pulled towards the black hole and trapped within it. If you start your own consultancy and do not run it correctly from a financial standpoint, you will be sucked into the black hole of financial hell with horrible speed. And not only will you be sucked into financial hell, but everything that was good about your life, and everyone who is dear to you, will also be sucked into it.

Yet, however powerful a force of dark attraction financial hell may be, if you inwardly digest and follow a few very basic and very important principles, you can be confident that you will never enter it.

These principles are as follows. I devote the remainder of this chapter to discussing them in detail.

1 Start your SFC with as little money as you possibly can and fund your SFC, from the outset, from the revenue that your SFC generates.
2 Never forget that you make money by not spending it.
3 Get the best price for your work that you possibly can.
4 Make sure you never have any bad debts.
5 Never pay yourself more than you can afford.

Set down on paper, these principles look obvious, even slightly banal. But if you regard them as such, that will be because you have never started and run your own consultancy and do not know the nature of the financial hazards – and temptations –

90

that are lying in wait for you, when you *do* start and run your own consultancy. If you were not fortunate enough to come across those five principles in this book and thus have the opportunity (which I hope you are wise enough to take) to assimilate them and carry them with you when you start your consultancy, you would have had to learn those principles for yourself during the first few years of your life as a consultant. You would almost certainly only learn those principles at the expenditure of much money and the suffering of much heartache, and it may well have been that, while spending that money and while suffering that heartache, you would have entered financial hell.

Fortunately, if you follow my advice, that need not happen. So let us examine in detail the five guiding principles which will lead you to financial heaven rather than hell.

91

1 START YOUR SFC WITH AS LITTLE MONEY AS YOU POSSIBLY CAN AND FUND YOUR SFC, FROM THE OUTSET, FROM THE REVENUE THAT YOUR SFC GENERATES

The importance of this fundamental principle is enshrined in the very term 'the self-fuelling consultancy'. The SFC is self-fuelling because it can be started – and indeed *should* be started – with the minimum of money, and once it has been started you should only fund it from the revenue that it is generating.

On the face of it, this advice is obvious, yet I have never seen this advice in any other business book that I have read apart from Paul Hawken's *Growing a Business*. Instead, the writers of most business books, when discussing the matter of funding, seem to regard their main task as giving their readers instructions for structuring a financial plan which they can then take to their bank manager in the hope of borrowing large amounts of money. Now, I have never started a factory such as a mousetrap factory and I have no idea whether anyone who plans to start a business like that really ought to start by going out and borrowing all the money needed to set up the factory, although I certainly have my doubts that this is the right way to proceed. But I have started and run my own consultancy, and I am absolutely certain that just about the worse thing you can do is start your consultancy by borrowing substantial amounts of money.

It is far, far better to start small, spending as little money as you can on your start-up and using your own money – even if you only have a little – to fund the start-up. As you saw in the last chapter, the basic practical requirements in terms of premises, equipment and stationery of a start-up SFC are relatively modest. Yes, I know that I told you to get yourself a decent chair and not to economise on stationery, but let's face it, those things aren't going to cost a king's ransom.

Only borrow money at all if it is *essential* that you do so. Borrow the minimum that you possibly can, and borrow it from your bank, not from some shady finance house which will charge you an extortionate rate of interest. Most important of all, when you are starting your SFC *don't* give your bank manager a lengthy and pompous financial plan. Your bank manager will have a long experience of assessing start-up businesses and will know that it is slightly ludicrous for a start-up consultancy to prepare a detailed financial plan; as the consultancy's start-up expenses should indeed be very low, and because what matters is not the financial plan but whether the consultancy can obtain clients on a sustained basis.

Instead of submitting a financial plan, go and see your bank manager and explain what you plan to do. It is important that he knows from the outset what your plans are; partly because he may have useful advice for you, and also because it is almost inevitable that at some point you will need a temporary over-draft facility and you will want to keep him sweet for when that happens.

If you *have* decided to ask him for a small loan, tell him that you're funding the start-up yourself (which ought to be true) but that you would like to borrow a couple of thousand pounds in order to get yourself (for example) a really comfortable chair to sit on, a brand new suit for meetings and some professional-looking stationery. Ask your bank manager to loan you the money for a 12-month period, with regular monthly re-payments. That way, during your first year of trading, the pain of having to make even those relatively small monthly re-payments should, with any luck, immunise you against ever wanting to take out a larger loan.

If you are contemplating borrowing more than a couple of thousand pounds from your bank manager, I strongly suspect that you are borrowing too much money and are, in fact, trying to set up a 'pretend' consultancy that is pretentious because its size is not directly related, from the outset, to its business volume. Go back to page 42, and read again my comments about 'pretend' consultancies.

There are three very important reasons why you should start your SFC with as little money as possible and only fund it from the revenue that it generates.

Firstly, *your financial risk will be minimised*, so that if your SFC does not develop as you hope you will have lost very little and will have the opportunity, if need be, to return to the salaried world without a huge burden of financial debt around your neck. The need to avoid the danger of indebtedness if your SFC does not work is important because, as I have already pointed out, you can never really be certain of what volume of business you will be able to achieve until you have actually gone out into the market and offered your services to potential clients.

Secondly, *your lack of money will make you hungry for success in order to make a living.* A surprisingly large number of business start-ups aim to borrow money (and sometimes succeed in doing so) on the basis of a financial plan which factors in, from the outset, a salary for the people who are running the business. Paying yourself a salary which you have borrowed from a bank seems to me such an absurd thing to do that it would hardly be worth my while taking the time to condemn this course of action, did not so many new businesses try to do it. If, on the other hand, you are in a position where you simply have to start earning money immediately or very soon, you will be very well motivated to make your SFC work – and make money for you – from the outset.

Thirdly, *you will be able to see the facts as soon as they arise, because your vision will not be clouded by too much money.* If you have too much money at the outset, there is a real danger that you may face the facts – such as that you do not really have the incremental advantage that you imagined yourself to have – much too late, and after you have spent (that is, wasted) far too much money. Similarly, if there *is* a real market for your services, but the nature of this market is not quite what you originally anticipated (such as a niche market which is more receptive to your services than the niche which you originally targeted), having too much money could lead you to pursue your original plans instead of meeting the needs of the real market. On the other hand, if you were hungry for business and strapped for cash, you would jump into that real market like a shot.

2 NEVER FORGET THAT YOU MAKE MONEY BY NOT SPENDING IT

Now onto the second of my five principles. This principle is also an extremely obvious one, but it, too, is frequently forgotten by people who are so caught up in the 'excitement' of starting a business that they lose the most elementary contact with financial reality.

In particular, many people who have hitherto exercised the most admirable prudence, self-control and good sense over their personal finances seem to lose all contact with restraint and a sense of reality when they start running a business. It is almost as if (or perhaps it is *exactly* as if) they thought that prudence, self-control and good sense are all very well when applied to one's own personal finances, but they are rather staid, unadventurous and boring qualities to bring to the world of business.

In fact, you need *more* prudence, self-control and good sense when managing the finances of a business than when managing your own finances, simply because there is likely to be much more money involved, with consequently worse results if things go wrong.

Indeed, by attributing this loss of control when running a business to a sense that financial control is boring and staid, I may be being kinder to people who display such loss of control than they deserve. In many cases, what is at the root of this loss of control is probably nothing more than a naive and foolish willingness to indulge in fantasies about all the money that the consultancy will make. Well, fair enough, I can't stop you indulging in fantasies if that is what you want to do. But if foolish fantasies are going to be guiding the financial management of your new consultancy, don't blame me if financial hell is just round the corner.

95

Put yourself into the frame of mind where you always remember that whenever you have avoided spending money, you have in effect made that money. If, for example, you are tempted to buy a large, brand new filing cabinet for £1,000 but then wisely decide to opt for an equally serviceable second-hand one for £500, say to yourself 'I have just made £500'. This is a highly effective discipline which will make you think twice about spending any money on your SFC that you absolutely do not need to spend.

3 GET THE BEST PRICE FOR YOUR WORK THAT YOU POSSIBLY CAN

We now move onto the exceedingly important question of pricing your services. There is no subtlety in the advice which I have for you in terms of your pricing; my guidance is straightforward and direct, and consists of the above guideline, which boils down to: *charge as much for your consultancy services as you can get away with*.

On the face of it this advice looks unscrupulous and even rather shady. But of course it is not, for the basic principle behind any business is that you should charge as much for what you are supplying as the market will bear, which is only a rather more genteel way of saying that you should charge as much as you can get away with.

Yes, I know that some business books tell you how to arrive at your pricing after due consideration of what it has cost you to make the product or provide the service, but such advice seems to me highly unrealistic, because it is ridiculous to imagine that price can be formulated on the basis of working out your costs, and adding to that a suitable sum for your own profits. Such an approach may have worked well at places such as Tractor Factory Number Fifteen in the former Soviet Union, where there were no market forces at work and where the economy was – at least in theory – planned at a central level. However, for you price is a dynamic quantity which is entirely a function of what the marketplace – that is, your clients – are prepared to pay for your services.

Of course, whether or not the price that your clients *are* prepared to pay for your services enables you to turn in a good profit on top of the expenses that you have incurred in order to make that service available, *is* a matter very much worth investigation.

I cannot tell you how much your clients will be prepared to pay you for your services, but I can tell you that as someone setting up a new consultancy, you may be in serious danger of pricing yourself out of the market if you have incurred great expense in arranging your start-up. Remember that as a new and – probably – small consultancy, competition over price is almost certainly going to be one of your important incremental advantages. Even if you regard the service that you are providing as being better than that which any large, well-known and well-established consultancy provides, you probably cannot price your service at that level. This is partly because your clients will know that your own overheads are much lower than a large consultancy's and will expect you to pass some of those lower overheads on to them, and partly because the client will, in effect, expect to be rewarded for trying you out as an unknown quantity, with that reward taking the form of lower fees than he would expect to pay if he had chosen to go to a better known consultancy.

Again, we see the importance of your start-up costs being minimised; so that you can charge a lower level of fees than your more established competitors will be charging.

Although ultimately the price that you can charge for your services is a function of what your particular marketplace will bear rather than what you decide you would like to earn, it is obviously helpful for you to estimate what it is costing you to run your consultancy. A good way of doing this is simply to come up with figures for what the following items cost you on a monthly basis:

- office rent;
- telephone and fax (but only including those telephone and fax charges which you cannot recover from your clients);
- heating and light;
- computer peripherals (e.g. ribbons, discs etc.).

Obviously, if you are working from home, the office rent should not be regarded as the monthly cost of your home mortgage or home rent. Instead, work out what percentage of your home is devoted to your office, and base your estimate of office rent on the relevant percentage of your total monthly mortgage or rent. If you do work at home, you should follow the same calculation procedure for telephone calls, heating and light, although your business telephone calls will probably be much more substantial than your domestic telephone calls.

Once you have worked out what the above items total in a month (the monthly operational cost), work out what fixed costs you have spent on equipment to set up the consultancy (e.g. chairs, word processors, fax machines etc.) and divide this by 12 to give you a putative monthly figure for your fixed costs. This approach involves you regarding yourself as paying for the equipment over a year, which may not necessarily be true, but which is a useful working assumption.

Note that all this is not anything to do with your proper accounting procedure, but simply a way for you to estimate what it costs you to run your consultancy each month.

Add the monthly operational cost to the one-twelfth of the fixed cost to get your estimate for running cost.

If you have followed the advice that I have given you so far in this book, the monthly cost of running your consultancy should easily allow you to undercut your larger competitors while still making an excellent profit for yourself and, as a consequence of that profit, giving yourself a high income.

While you should bear in mind the dangers of overcharging, you must also not forget that it is both foolish and dangerous to undercharge for your services.

98

Not only will undercharging have the result that you will not be properly rewarded for your initiative in setting up an SFC and in working hard to meet your clients' needs, but there is a real danger that if you charge too little for your services, your existing and/or potential clients will not regard you with the respect that they ought to regard you. This is because one of the aspects of the relatively complex psychology which is at work when clients hire a consultant (I have more to say about this psychology in the next chapter) is that clients regard the act of employing a consultant as boosting their own status in the business world. If the consultant pitches his fees too low, the client will feel that the consultant is perhaps not a very good one, will feel their ego insufficiently boosted, and may be unwilling to hire the consultant.

You have to be aware of this aspect of psychology, and act with it in mind. Ultimately, what this means is that you must have the courage and confidence in the expertise that you are offering via your SFC to avoid charging too little for your services.

So what exactly should you be charging your clients? While there can be no hard and fast rule about this, since obviously I do not know the commercial or industrial sector in which you are operating, I would say, other things being equal, that in the first year of the operation of your consultancy you should not be charging less than £300 per day for your time, or, if you are working with fellow consultants, that none of you should charge out your services at less than £300 per day. Ideally you should aim to charge between £400 to £500 per day for your consultancy time, but it may be that in the first year of your consultancy's operation this figure is a somewhat over-optimistic one. However, if you can get away with it, by all means do so.

You will, certainly, have to develop an awareness of the market rate for consultancy services in your particular sector and bear that in mind when you fix your prices. Remember, too, that ultimately you can charge whatever you like for your consultancy services, and that you do not necessarily need to charge different clients the same rate. There is no reason why you should not charge larger, well-established clients more than you charge smaller, less well-established clients. In any event, by the time you get round to starting your SFC, the five years of experience which, if you have followed my suggestion, you will already have in your chosen specialisation, will most likely have given you a good knowledge of what consultants who work in your specialisation usually charge. Even if it has not, you will probably know how to find out this information.

99

Should you or should you not undercut the going rate for consultancy services in your sector? This will depend, again, on whether you think you can get away with it. Even if you have anticipated that price competition is going to be one of your incremental advantages, the fact remains that there is no point charging a client less than you can get away with. You will simply have to use your own experience and knowledge, combined with – I hope – some of the ideas that I have already set down in this chapter.

As should be clear from the above, I recommend that your pricing be based around quoting a daily rate for your consultancy's services. Some consultants and consultancies quote an hourly rate to clients and multiply this by 8 to get a daily rate, but I have never really seen much point in quoting an hourly rate, since no consultant worth his salt is going to take on a project which is worth less than one day of his time.

You can offer your services in two ways: either on a *project* basis (this is also often called an ad hoc basis), where you work out in advance how many days of your time a particular project will require and agree with your client a fee based on that number of days; or a *retainer* basis, where you agree to work for your client for a certain number of days every month.

The option that you choose will depend on the type of project that you are carrying out. If you are undertaking a project which has a definite beginning, middle and end (such as a review of the effectiveness of some aspect of your client's resources, with this review taking the form of a report to be written once you have completed your field research), then it will probably be most effective for you to charge on a project basis. If, on the other hand, you are entrusted with a particular activity on an ongoing basis, it makes more sense to charge on a retainer basis. For example, a large part of my own activity as a consultant is the generation of press coverage for my clients, and I find it much more helpful to charge for this service on a retainer basis than on a project basis.

When you choose the retainer option, the question naturally arises for how many months at a stretch you should ask your client to agree to hire you. In my own specialised field, public relations, many consultancies require clients to hire the consultancy for a minimum period of one year when consultancy services are provided on a retainer basis.

I admit that there is something in the arguments which the consultancies use to justify this requirement to themselves and to their clients. One principal argument is that the consultancy will have to devote resources – perhaps even recruit new personnel – in order to service the account and will need to have a fairly lengthy sustained contract for retainer service if the account is to be profitable. The second argument is that it will take time for editorial coverage generated by the consultancy's activity to be published, and if the contractual period is too short, the client may not have the opportunity of seeing the tangible published results of what the consultancy is doing for it.

Even given the validity of these arguments, a new consultancy which insisted on offering its services on a 'one-year minimum contract' basis might quickly find that it had imposed a condition which was preventing it from obtaining much in the way of business. As a new, untried consultancy, your SFC cannot simply impose its conditions on its marketplace, but must earn the right to request those conditions by achieving real results for its clients and thereby creating a reservoir of client goodwill and an ample supply of – to use Paul Hawken's phrase – 'permission of the marketplace'.

101

On the other hand, taking on a client for a retainer period of a couple of months is not likely to benefit either you, or your client.

I therefore suggest that you seek to work with your clients on a retainer basis of a *minimum period of six months*. That way, not only will you give your prospective clients the confidence that they can take you on without hemming themselves into a year-long agreement, but you yourself will have the incentive to work really hard and really effectively for your client during those six months, *so that your client is not only prepared to renew the agreement after six months, but is positively enthusiastic about doing so.*

There are some final points which I want to make in relation to your approach to pricing. These points are not usually covered in business books, but I have found them of great practical importance when running my own consultancy.

Pricing approach – further points

i *Deciding how many hours to charge*

Remember that just because you are charging a client for a day's work as a consultant, you do not *necessarily* need to spend a full eight hours on the task in hand. As a consultant, you are being hired for *what you can achieve*, not for the number of hours that you devote to a project. What matters is how *effective* you are, and if, as you grow more experienced as a consultant, your increasing expertise means that you can achieve in three hours what other consultants (or you, six months ago) could only achieve in eight hours, *and if the client is prepared to pay you a day's fee for those three hours* (given that you will not, of course, tell him that you achieved eight hours' worth of effect in three hours of work) then so much the better for you.

102

ii *Over-servicing*

Be careful to avoid *over-servicing* your clients. While you must, of course, work hard from the outset to keep your clients happy and to maximise the likelihood that they want you to work for them in the future, there is a real danger that in your enthusiasm to make your SFC a success, you give your clients *too much* value for money; that is, you devote more time and effort to their interests than is required by the agreement into which you have entered with them.

The drawback with doing this is that the client will come to expect you to keep up the same level of over-servicing for all the time that you are working for them, with the result not only that this particular client's account will not be very profitable for you, but also that you may neglect your other clients as well as opportunities which may arise for the winning of new business.

iii *A contingency for additional work*

Similarly, when you agree to work for a client on an ad hoc basis, you *must* have a provision in the agreement for what happens if (as usually *does* happen) the client makes additional demands on you not covered by the original agreement, or if it becomes clear (and again, it often does) that the client did not fully clarify the complexity of the project at the outset; although to some extent you can guard against this danger by being quite certain, before you quote for the project, regarding what work needs to be undertaken.

I suggest you include in the agreement a provision that additional days of activity will be charged on a pro rata basis, but that you will only undertake any additional work if you receive *written* permission from the client to do so. You need written permission because – as I once discovered to my cost – it is all too easy, in the heat of the moment and when the client is under pressure to get the job done, for one of the client's managerial staff to ask you to do the additional work required and then, when you have solved the problem for the client, for the client to turn round and say that you have overcharged them.

iv *Charging expenses at cost*

When you make agreements with clients, charge out-of-pocket expenses (e.g. your telephone and fax charges, postage, rail fares etc.) to them *at cost* rather than (as many consultancies do) adding a fixed percentage to the expense (this fixed percentage is called the 'mark-up') when invoicing.

The small amount of additional revenue which you will lose from not imposing a mark-up will be vastly outweighed by the goodwill that this aspect of your pricing policy will create for you with your clients.

Note that this advice does *not* apply with major expenses that you may incur on a client's behalf. For example, if you have arranged for the printing of a brochure for your client, it would be foolish for you not to mark up the printing cost, as this mark-up is a legitimate way for you to be compensated for the slight risk (and it *should* be slight – see below) of incurring an expense on a client's behalf. The mark-up is also your reward for having taken the trouble to liaise with the printer, although the time expended here will also be covered by your fee. Your mark-up should be in the vicinity of 15 per cent.

Note that for advertising agencies – which are in their own way a form of advertising consultancy – the mark-up on media spend is an important part of the revenue deriving from a particular client, even though advertising agencies are increasingly using fee-based structures, in addition to the mark-up.

v *Travelling time*

Do not forget that time spent *travelling* on a client's behalf is time for which you can legitimately charge, although you do have to use tact and discretion here to avoid annoying your clients.

Many kinds of projects that you undertake for a client could not be completed without time spent travelling. For example, if you were visiting a certain number of your client's offices around the country, you would naturally expect your client to pay for the travelling time that you expend on travelling from your own base to the first of your client's offices, and then from the first to the second office, and so on.

Similarly, if you live an hour or so's journey time from your client's office and you have to go to the client's office for a meeting which lasts two hours, it would be perfectly legitimate for you to regard this as half a day of your time.

The only problem that arises here is when you are making a passing visit to your client's offices, such as to drop off a document or pick something up. I really do recommend that you show some sensitivity and tact here, particularly if – as may well be the case – you have other clients located in the vicinity and are also visiting them. In such cases you should be scrupulously ethical and only charge the travelling time to one client, or consider not charging travelling time at all if you were in the vicinity anyway, such as for a shopping trip or a visit to the theatre.

Only charge travelling time when you have genuinely and

completely made the journey purely on the client's behalf. Following this rule may cause you occasionally to lose out on some travel time, but your client will appreciate your honesty and will, with any luck, bear it in mind when next thinking about whether to give you some further work, or whether to renew your retainer contract.

You will, of course, charge the *expenses* of your travelling to the client; whether these are the train fare, air fare or an agreed petrol cost.

vi *Timing of invoices*

Remember that proper timing of the despatch of your invoices is essential to your cash flow and consequent general morale. I recommend that you adopt the following approach to the timing of your invoices.

105

For ad hoc projects, if you are dealing with a large and well-established client organisation which you regard as being an extremely good credit risk, *invoice the total agreed fee for the project when you have completed half the number of agreed days*. That way, by the time you have finished the entire project, you should be well on your way to being paid.

If, on the other hand, you are about to undertake an ad hoc project for a client organisation which you only regard as a moderately good credit risk, *invoice for 50 per cent of the fee AND all the planned expenses (i.e. disbursements) before you start the project and do not start work until you receive this money and until the cheque clears*. If the client will not do this, do not work for them. After all, if the client is not willing (or cannot afford) to pay you for your planned disbursements and half your fee *before* you start the project, is there any reason to assume that they would be willing to pay you (or be able to afford to pay you) your expenses and the full fee once you have *completed* the project?

When invoicing for retainer projects, I recommend you invoice in full the fee for a particular month's work *at the beginning of the month in which you will be doing the work*.

This sounds pushy, but in fact it is not, since even if the client pays you within 30 days, you will only be getting paid by the end of the month in which you do the work i.e. after you have done the work. If the client takes longer than 30 days to pay you, you will still receive your payment within a reasonable period after completing the work for that month.

On the other hand, if you do not invoice until the *end* of the month in which you are doing the work, even if the client takes only 30 days to pay you, you will still not get paid until at least a month after you have completed the work. In the meantime, you will have done another month's work, so that you are always at least two lots of one month's work behind in terms of getting paid. It is not in your interests to do business in this way.

I have never found that clients object to being presented at the start of a month with an invoice for that month, as long as they know from the outset that this is how I do business. After all, submitting an invoice to them in this way does not put any immediate pressure on them to pay you, it simply means that – as your clients will most likely decide when to pay you on the basis of when they received your invoice rather than when you did the work – you will be a month ahead, in terms of receiving payment, on any system which involves invoicing them a month later.

vii *The need to avoid errors*

Take care not to make any numerical errors on your invoices, whether these errors relate to the amounts you are charging under different headings, your adding-up of the various amounts, or to your calculations of any additions to the invoice deriving from the imposition of statutory taxes.

Remember that if you make errors on your invoices you run the risk either of charging your client less than you are due (and it is not always easy to rectify this problem by sending another invoice without annoying the client), or charging your client more than you are due, when the client will almost certainly query the invoice, thereby delaying your payment.

viii *Timesheets*

Once you start working for several clients, you may find it easier to prepare invoices if you have kept a record of when you worked for a particular client, how much time you spent on them, and what you did. Although, as I have said, I do not see much point in charging clients in units of less than a day of your time. The fact is that if you have several clients it is likely that on days when you are working in your office you will be acting on behalf of more than one client during a day. It can sometimes be useful for your own records to keep what is known as a 'timesheet' for each client. This is simply a record of the hours you spend on a particular client's behalf on the various days during a specific month. You can then add up all the hours that you spend and invoice the number of hours, as well as keep tabs on whether you are under- or over-servicing a client's account.

107

In practice, however, timesheets are only really of much use where you reach the stage of employing (or working with) numerous other consultants, and want to find out exactly how they are spending their time. When you are working alone, or perhaps with one or two other people, timesheets don't really help you very much *because what you are selling as a consultant is ultimately not your time but your effectiveness*. Once you become skilled in what you do (which is an evolutionary process when you start your own consultancy even if you began your consultancy with a good deal of experience in your chosen field) you will find that you can achieve more and more in a shorter time. This being the case, there is a real danger that you will sell yourself short if you stick rigorously to charging your clients for the precise hours and minutes that you work on their behalf. What you really need to do is, in effect, charge them for as much time as you feel they are prepared to accept that a particular job will take you to do, which may *not* necessarily be the amount of time that the job *actually required*.

This, as I have mentioned already, is not deceitful, since the crucial factor here is that the client is happy with the amount of time that you are claiming a task took you to undertake.

Rather, it is good business practice, and will lead to your consultancy maximising its profitability, which is, after all, the idea.

Of course, any time that you do charge your clients will have to conform to what you have already agreed with them. Where you need to go beyond what you have already agreed, make sure – as I said – that the client agrees to the additional time and consequent additional expenses before you begin the additional work.

Incidentally, once you reach the stage where you are employing numerous consultants and where timesheets are an important means for you to keep track of what is going on in your consultancy, remember that you are not the only person who may be completing timesheets on the basis of what you think you can get away with, rather than according to what work you have actually completed.

108

ix *Making your invoices acceptable*

Finally, bear in mind the most important rule of invoicing: *never send an invoice unless you are completely confident that your client is expecting to receive it.*

Like many of the most important rules in this book, this rule is very simple and straightforward, but is too often ignored. In fact, there really is no other way to run the invoicing side of your SFC than to have a policy of never sending out invoices which will distress your clients.

Far too many businesses – particularly businesses run by professional advisers such as lawyers, accountants and consultants – send out invoices which are either larger than the client is expecting or (worse still) which the client is not expecting to receive at all.

I think that businesses which do this are either being run by fools, or else – which may be less forgiveable – are being run by people who are so arrogant that they actually think, more or less, that their clients should consider themselves privileged to receive the invoice.

Believe me, no client ever considers himself privileged to receive an invoice, even if the invoice is accurate and is what he expected. Where the invoice is either too high or is unexpected, the client will feel nothing but annoyance and contempt for you. Even if he does pay up, that is the last that you will see of him.

There is absolutely no reason at all to send a client an invoice which he is not expecting to receive unless you are foolish enough not to agree precise terms with your client before starting work with him, or otherwise inconsiderate of your clients, in which case the money that you spent on this book has been wasted.

4 MAKE SURE YOU NEVER HAVE ANY BAD DEBTS

When you go to your local supermarket and stock up on groceries, you have to pay for these groceries at the check-out. True, if you decide to pay for the groceries by credit card or charge card you will enjoy (if that is the right word) the privilege of, in effect, actually paying for the goods at a later date, but the payment transaction must none the less take place there and then, at the check-out. You certainly cannot breezily give the check-out person your name and address, and ask them to send you an invoice which you will pay at some unspecified later date.

That, however, is precisely how the world of commerce operates, and you have to live with it.

When you start your SFC you will presumably be used to paying for most things as and when you receive them. Even your former salary was presumably paid on a regular basis on a specific day.

It can be quite a shock to many people who start their own SFCs to discover that an invoice is a bill which the recipient basically has the option of paying as and when he wishes to.

In other words, you are going to be doing business in an

109

environment where the general rule is that services are provided on credit.

I may as well say right now that there is no doubt that the whole area of giving credit is one of the biggest causes of anxiety and difficulty to anyone who sets up a business of any kind, whether or not that business is a consultancy.

In theory and to some extent also in practice, the types of business which suffer most from extending credit are manufacturing businesses which must perforce accrue the cost of raw materials before they can produce any goods. If their customers do not pay up, insolvency is never far away.

However, even though – as someone running a consultancy – you should be able to supply your services without having to accrue large financial commitments in order to do so, you will still have incurred fixed costs in setting up your consultancy, and there will, of course, also be your regular operational costs to pay. Your financial risk in trading may not be as great as that accrued by a manufacturing company, but you still cannot afford to work without getting paid for what you do.

In fact, although most people regard a 'bad debt' as a debt that is never recoverable, in my own thinking and practice I regard bad debts as also consisting of debts that are not *readily* recoverable: which includes debts that are only paid after you have initiated legal action against the debtor, or debts that are only paid many months (say, more than six months) after you have completed the relevant work.

Now, I do not think that there are *too* many junctures in this book when I can be accused of blowing my own trumpet, but it is a simple and truthful fact that, in the almost six years that I have been trading as a consultant, during which time I have issued almost 500 invoices, I have never suffered any debts that are bad debts according to the above definition. I have, on two occasions, had to commence legal proceedings against a client due to non-payment of an invoice. In both of these instances, the matters were settled out of court, with me settling for a lower amount than was on the invoice. In both cases I believe that the invoice which I initially sent was fair and reasonable, based on what I had agreed with the clients, but I was prepared to accept a lower fee in order to settle the matter.

On another occasion a client went bust owing me payment for about five days of consultancy time, but fortunately the people who had run the organisation which went bust wanted to use my services again when they set up a new company, and I refused to work for them again until they had paid me most of what they owed me, and they did pay me this.

I think it is reasonable to conclude from my own experience as a consultant that bad debts need not become a part of your own activities in running an SFC. I certainly do not believe that bad debts are an inevitable consequence of being in business. I think that people who have come to believe this are making certain obvious mistakes in how they run their business.

111

You must, from the outset, resolve to avoid accruing bad debts if you possibly can. Bad debts are very, very bad news. Not only is it disastrous for your morale to accrue bad debts, but it is literally better to go fishing, watch television or stay in bed rather than undertake work for which you will not be paid, since you will have incurred expenses in carrying out that work which you would not have incurred if you had not done the work. You should also bear in mind that the cost of a bad debt to you is not only the expenses that you incurred by carrying out the work but also the revenue that you would have earned if you had devoted the time to working for a client who *will* pay you. Economists call this cost 'opportunity cost'.

Accruing bad debts is a particular danger when you are just starting to run an SFC, because in your eagerness to win and work on business there is a real hazard that you may work for clients whose ability to pay you is questionable. In fact, you may even have strong reasons to suspect that their ability to pay you is in doubt, but you may be willing to work for them none the less. After all, they *might* pay you.

They probably won't.

They probably won't, because they will almost certainly be perfectly aware that you are a start-up and that, as a result, you will be hungry for new business. Some organisations are only too happy to exploit such a hunger.

In the above case, your prospective client is simply behaving unscrupulously, but there are also many prospective clients who, while not inherently dishonest or unethical, are incompetent businessmen who cannot manage their financial affairs. We can call this the 'Mr Micawber' syndrome, where your client *wants* to pay you, may indeed passionately want to pay you; may be tearful that he cannot, at this moment, pay you; but cannot pay you, all the same.

You don't need to be a financial genius to see that, for you as a consultant, the financial result is the same whether your client is being deliberately unscrupulous or is merely incompetent. The result, in either case, is that you don't get your money, or else get it so late that the benefits to you of having worked on this particular piece of business have long been eroded.

Taking bad debtors to court is never a good idea unless there is absolutely no alternative, and I firmly state this despite having, as I said, managed to recover some money from two bad debts once I initiated court proceedings.

For one thing, taking people or firms to court will involve you in some expense. Although many jurisdictions nowadays have local courts which can process routine summons for non-payment relatively quickly and at fairly low expense, you will still need to risk that expense and if you fail to recover any money you will have to bear that expense.

More to the point, though, taking people or firms to court is horribly worrying, horribly boring, very dismal and depressing and – worst of all – time-consuming.

Most business books talk about taking people to court to recover debts as if it were some normal part of the debt collection business. Well, maybe it is for the people who write the average business book, but it should not be for *you. For you,*

112

taking your clients to court should absolutely be the last resort, if for no other reason than the whole spirit of a successful SFC depends on forging relationships with clients that generate business and mutual goodwill for many years, whereas if you take a client to court you will almost certainly never work with them again.

How to avoid accruing bad debts

As with many other areas covered in this book, I believe that the procedure for avoiding accruing bad debts can, to some extent, be taught, although – and this, too, is also true for other areas in this book – the principles which I advise you to follow are only a starting point, and will need to be fleshed out by your own experience and business sense.

Here, anyway, are my suggestions for how to avoid accruing bad debts. I have six suggestions, and I have ranked them in what I believe is the descending order of their importance.

113

i *Before you start working for a client, obtain a signed written agreement which specify what activity or activities you will be undertaking for your client, and how much your client will be paying you.*

This is the most fundamental way to protect yourself against accruing bad debts. If everything is written down, a client will be much less likely to baulk on payment. There is also the important point that the client's memory of what was agreed may simply be faulty, and once you are able to show the client the written agreement they will be perfectly happy to pay you.

You do not necessarily need to draw up long-winded agreements which will frighten your clients off; indeed I firmly believe that such agreements are a threat to the goodwill which should exist between you and your client from the outset. I suggest a format for informal but effective client agreements – both for ad hoc and retainer projects – in Chapter 6.

Incidentally, there's not much point in obtaining signed written agreements unless you file them where they can be easily retrieved and hold onto them until the job has been completed and paid for.

ii *Before you start working for a client, make sure that the client knows exactly how much you will be invoicing, and when.*

Although in theory this information should be included in the written agreement, it might not be, and even if it is, the client might not be aware of the precise financial consequences of what will be happening. Make sure that the client is precisely aware of these consequences. That way, you will avoid giving him any nasty surprises.

iii *If you have reason to doubt that a client will be able to afford to pay you, ask to be paid your fee and expenses before you start work.*

Generally speaking, clients who are bad payers look as if they might be. Their offices are tatty, their staff are demoralised and do a lot of complaining, phone calls take a long time to be answered and the client himself is full of grandiose plans but doesn't seem to have achieved much to date.

Beware such clients, for almost every consultant encounters them at some point or another. They want your assistance so that they can use it to make money, but they don't see why you should complain if you don't get paid for six months, if at all.

Don't work for such clients without first having received the fee and expenses upfront (and waited until the cheque has cleared). If they refuse to go along with this, don't bother working for them.

Ignore this advice at your peril.

It is true that you can (for a fee) obtain details of a particular firm's credit record from a credit reference agency, but this information only tells you what a firm's credit record has been like to date; it doesn't tell you what they're going to be like as payers *in the future.*

Besides, bad payers know all about credit reference agencies, and are forever creating new firms which are too new to have a bad credit record.

iv *Never lay out anything but a minimal amount of money on expenses resulting from working on a client's behalf.*

It should be patently obvious that one excellent way for a new consultancy (or a long-established consultancy) to descend into financial hell with great rapidity is to lay out a considerable amount of money on a client's behalf (or accrue debts) and not to get reimbursed for the money.

No room for compromise here. *Never* – and I mean never, because making this mistake just once can wipe you out – incur anything but a minimal expense (say, up to around £250 maximum) on a client's behalf *without having cleared funds in your bank account from the client to cover the expense.*

115

No ifs, no buts, no special cases. Even if it's last thing on Friday and you need to get things moving and the client says you'll have the money first thing on Monday. *Get that money upfront.* Don't be rushed into a financial commitment which you may regret for ever.

v *Let your relationships with clients be infused with goodwill.*

Other things being equal, a client who likes you and respects you will treat you fairly and pay you on time. Even where a client is doing badly financially, if he likes you and respects you he will give you ample warning of any imminent possible difficulty in paying; thereby giving you the opportunity either to stop working for the client completely or else to reduce the amount of work that you do for him.

vi *Make it your policy to request that your invoices be paid within 30 days of submitting them, and do your utmost to ensure that your clients adhere to this.*

Requesting payment within 30 days is entirely reasonable for a consultancy which is supplying skills provided by people who are making their living from providing that expertise. Even if your clients have a policy of paying their other suppliers after a longer credit period, you can almost always get your clients to accept your own credit terms, if you are firm but polite, and if they really want to work with you. If a client refuses to accept your terms, ask yourself whether the client is really worth working for. Having invoices paid only after 60 or 90 days will give you horrendous cash flow problems unless you have substantial capital in the bank. I would not advise you to accept these payment terms unless your client is a large, well-known, ultra-creditworthy organisation which, apart from the money that you will finally earn from them, it will be greatly in the interests of your consultancy's status to have on your client list.

116

Now onto the final point regarding how to manage the financial side of your SFC.

5 NEVER PAY YOURSELF MORE THAN YOU CAN AFFORD

Do I need to say anything here other than that you should aim to restrict your cash drawings from your SFC to what your SFC can bear, given that you should keep a surplus sum in the consultancy's bank account in order to cover contingencies?

What this surplus should be is entirely up to you, but I strongly advise you to make sure that you have a surplus in place. As the great English poet Alexander Pope said, 'Hope springs eternal in the human breast' and one somewhat unfortunate consequence of this facet of human nature is that we often view our financial prospects with more optimism than is warranted. As a result, we are frequently unprepared when financial reversals take place.

A financial reversal need not necessarily consist of a reduction in your revenue such as is occasioned by one of your largest clients going bust; it can just as easily consist of an unexpected drain on your resources such as a sudden health problem which must be attended to, or your twenty-year old son writing to you from Katmandu prison, from which he urgently needs to be bailed.

In any event, make sure that you have a financial surplus at all times in your SFC's bank account, and do not overdo the personal drawings, particularly in the early days when you are not yet sure that a very good second month (for example) will not be followed by a dreadful third and fourth month.

I conclude this chapter with some comments on three general issues relating to the management of the financial affairs of an SFC.

Dealing with indebtedness 117

Just as you need to be rigorously on your guard to avoid accruing bad debts, you must also take every step to avoid incurring debts yourself which you are not able to pay within the time limits requested by your suppliers, or within statutory time limits in the case of official payments such as for tax.

Not only is being on the receiving end of letters requesting payment and demands for payment seriously demoralising, but you will frequently incur additional expenses such as interest payments and even financial penalties in the case of late payments of statutory debts.

The way to avoid incurring debts which you cannot readily pay is to follow my advice about remembering that you make money by not spending it. You should also plan sufficiently ahead so that you can be very confident that you will have ample revenue at a certain time in order to fund a payment that you have to make.

Having said all this, even the best-run consultancies sometimes find that they have incurred debts which they cannot easily pay within the creditor's normal credit period. If you find yourself in this position, the golden rule is: *explain your position to the creditor immediately and keep them informed of what you are doing.*

The vast majority of creditors – including, by the way, government offices – will be happy to give you extra time to pay, given that you have taken the trouble to contact them and are sincere about clearing the debt.

What creditors cannot abide is where a debtor simply does not have the courtesy to contact them and where the debtor ignores letters and demands which the creditor sends.

Generally, if you make the effort to let the creditor know what is happening and reassure the creditor that you will be able to pay the debt, albeit at a somewhat later date, most creditors will be only too pleased that you have taken the initiative to contact them.

118

However, important as communicating with your creditors is when you have temporary difficulty in settling a debt, communication is not going to be of much avail if you have managed your SFC's financial affairs so badly that you will not be able to settle the outstanding debt in the foreseeable future. However, if you have followed my advice about starting small and growing in response to market demand rather than in response to your own ambitions, if you have sought to minimise your expenditure on your SFC, and if you have taken every step to avoid accruing bad debts yourself, there is absolutely no reason at all why you should descend into the financial hell of having debts which you cannot pay.

Insurance

Before you start trading, you will need to make sure that you have all the appropriate statutory insurances in place, as well as having in place all optional insurances that you will need.
You will require professional advice here, so go to an insurance broker and find out which insurances you are obliged to have, and which insurances you ought to have.

My own recommendations for optional insurance are that you insure all your office equipment against all kinds of hazards including fire and theft. A start-up consultancy could be killed off in its early days if all its office equipment was damaged or stolen and if no insurances were in place to fund the purchase of new equipment. Incidentally, make sure that your insurance cover, if invoked, will enable you to buy the same equipment that you had before; not cheaper versions of this.

You should also consider the option of taking out an insurance policy which will provide you with an income in the event of you suffering a serious illness or an accident and therefore being unable to work. Remember that if you are running your own SFC and are unable to work, you may rapidly find yourself with no income whatsoever.

You will also probably want to take out life insurance, so that your dependants will have some capital if you die suddenly. Check the status of any life insurance that you had when working for your last employer: it may be that this will have lapsed when you left your job.

You will probably already have effective medical insurance in place, but if you do not, get some now. Should you fall ill and require an operation, you will not want to hang around on a waiting list, but you will want to have the job done as quickly as possible so that you can get back to work with the minimum delay.

Choosing an accountant

Unless you are an accountant by profession, I strongly advise you to find an accountant who will prepare accounts for you and undertake other tasks which you are obliged to carry out, such as prepare tax returns and deal with any tax affairs that must be dealt with on an ongoing basis.

I do *not* advise you to try to do this work yourself. You should be devoting all your work time to carrying out projects for your existing clients and winning new ones; not to undertaking accounting work which is better entrusted to a professional.

However, this advice does not, of course, mean that I advise you to be reckless about what you pay for accountancy services. In particular, large accountancy firms are very unlikely to be much use to you. They are (probably) geared up to working for far larger clients than you, with the result that your work will either be entrusted to some junior who will be unable to give you any proper advice when you need it, or else you will be given services that you do not really need and will be charged exorbitantly for the privilege. Small, local accountancy firms may be worth considering, but often their fees are scarcely any lower than what large firms charge.

The solution to this dilemma is to find yourself a freelance accountant who will work hard and efficiently for you for only a moderate fee. You can, of course, expect to pay a moderate fee, because a freelance accountant, like a start-up SFC, ought only to have minimal overheads.

So how do you find such a person? The trouble with simply looking through business directories is that some freelance accountants are freelance because they are either incompetent or crooked, and no business directory will tell you whether the accountant that you are thinking of using fits into these categories.

Probably the best way to obtain a good freelance accountant is through the personal recommendation of someone you trust. Failing this, a good ruse is to telephone an accountancy firm (large or small) in your locality, explain to them that you have just started a business and have only a very limited budget for accountancy costs, and ask them if any of their partners have recently retired and might be interested in doing some occasional freelance work. This approach may bring results, or perhaps the firm will take pity on you and find someone within the firm who will do for you only the minimum that needs to be done and charge you a correspondingly low fee, but who will be on hand to give you useful professional advice about business-related matters when you need this advice.

5

How to make your clients think you're wonderful

Introduction

As a consultant, your working relationships with your clients are the most valuable assets you possess. Even if you have followed my advice and have resolved to start your SFC small, grow organically in response to demand and minimise your expenditure at every stage of your development, merely following these key precepts will only create the conditions which make success possible; they will not of themselves lead to success. In the final analysis, it is only the quality of your working relationships with your clients which will bring you the professional and financial success to which you aspire.

Ultimately, the way to have quality relationships with your clients is to work *hard*, *effectively* and *sincerely* on your clients' behalf. Working hard is insufficient if you are not also effective, and you can only be truly effective if you have a sincere empathy for your client's aims. The reason you are working hard, effectively and sincerely on your clients' behalf is so that you can help them to become more successful. This fundamental aim is (or at least, should be) the prime objective of a consultant's activities on behalf of his clients, and there is no short cut to this objective.

If you work hard, effectively and sincerely on your clients' behalf, and make their success your fundamental objective, you will reap the financial rewards for doing this, and you will keep on reaping them.

And, yes, it is perfectly acceptable for you to make your own financial success an important private aim of your own, but you will only achieve that financial success on a sustained basis if you make your *primary* aim the provision of expert assistance to your clients to make them more successful.

Unfortunately for the consultancy profession, there are some consultants who do not make their clients' success their primary aim, but instead seek to gain short-term financial benefits from a client by devious means such as getting the client to sign a contract which has the effect of bringing the consultant very considerable revenue for a minimum amount of work. Because clients are sometimes rather intimidated by consultants – particularly consultants with expensive-looking suits and pompous voices – clients will, on occasion, sign these contracts and enrich the consultant in return for very little tangible benefit to the client. However, consultants who operate in this way tend to be a dying breed, and rightly so, because clients who feel that they have been taken for a ride by a consultant will certainly never use the services of that consultant again, and will make sure that their business associates will be quite aware of the dirty deeds that the consultant in question perpetrated.

Taking clients for a ride is no way to run a successful high-income consultancy. Instead, you must make every effort to ensure that, from the very first moment when they come in contact with you to the time (perhaps many years later) when you part company, your clients are convinced of your remarkable talents, your professionalism, your hard work and your utter dedication to their interests.

In this chapter I take you, step-by-step, through the process of making an initial contact with clients, starting to get professionally involved with clients, and working for clients on an ongoing basis, so that at every stage you see how you can work so as to gain maximum respect and admiration from your clients.

Although some of the business practices that I recommend

consist of what are essentially tactical measures, underlying everything is the fundamental requirement to work hard, effectively and sincerely. I can teach you some useful business practices to maximise the esteem in which your clients hold you, but I cannot teach you how to work hard, effectively and sincerely. That is something that you must learn for yourself, although I certainly believe that the two secrets of working in this way are, firstly, to love the area of specialisation in which you are working and, secondly, to gain pleasure from looking after a client's interests and from seeing the benefits which your work has on a client's business.

The most important guiding principle of all

123

Before moving onto my step-by-step analysis of how to gain maximum respect and admiration from your clients, I want to introduce a fundamental principle which should underlie every single aspect of your dealings with your clients, whether these clients are business prospects or clients with whom you have been working for many years.

The principle is this: *seek at every stage to imagine yourself in your client's shoes.*

In other words, practise the discipline of looking at every situation from your client's perspective. You should teach yourself to do this so frequently that in the end it becomes an instinctive action. If you do this, and do it properly and sincerely, you will be well on the way to giving real client satisfaction *because you will always genuinely be able to see situations, dynamics and problems from their perspective as well as from your own.*

Above all, the discipline of looking at situations from your client's point of view will very soon force you to realise that *your own priorities and time-frames are not your client's priorities and time-frames.* If more consultants took the trouble to bear this in mind, a very high proportion of the problems which consultants have with their clients would never happen. Instead, the clients would regard their consultants as considerate, fair and intelligent.

Note that what I most emphatically am *not* suggesting here is that you should agree with your client at every point. Putting yourself in your client's shoes and understanding that your own priorities and time-frames are not your client's priorities and time-frames is something very different from agreeing with whatever your client says. Instead, putting yourself in your client's shoes is a mental discipline which allows you to see (as far as you can know this) what is motivating your client to think and act as he does. Not only will this mental discipline greatly assist you to conduct an amicable and mutually beneficial relationship with your client, but on those occasions when you have to disagree with your client – whether over an aspect of your relationship or when in the course of your work as a consultant you advise them against a particular course of action that they want to pursue – the client will listen hard to the reasons why you disagree with them.

Let us now proceed to my step-by-step guide to making your clients think that you're wonderful.

Step 1: the initial contact with clients

You must ensure that ultra-professionalism and a very high degree of ability infuse your relationships with your clients from the very first contact with them. In practice, this means that you must pay particular attention to your initial telephone calls to your clients, and also to the initial letters that you write to them. Note that the advice which I have regarding telephone calls and letters holds good for telephone calls which you make to your clients and letters which you send them once you have established a good working relationship. However, this advice is particularly important for the initial stages of your involvement with your clients.

TELEPHONE CALLS

If your first contact with a client is by telephone and you are initiating the call (for example, an existing client might have spoken to your prospective client who has requested that you call them), make sure – before you phone – that you are *absolutely certain* how to spell the name of the prospective client organisation and the name of the person you will be telephoning.

Also, before you pick up that receiver, make sure that you have worked out what the objective of the telephone conversation is. If it is to introduce yourself to the client and to seek to arrange a meeting, keep the conversation confined to those two objectives. The prospective client does not want to know about all the problems you have suffered since you started your SFC. At a later stage, as and when you have established a mutually beneficial working relationship with your client, there may be room for more personal types of conversation, but not now.

125

The above guidelines are just two of my guidelines for being professional on the telephone. Generally, my recommendations for this are as follows:

- Know how to spell the name of the client organisation and the client contact before you telephone.

- Work out what the objective of the telephone conversation is before you telephone, and stick to that objective.

- Leave out any personal talk in the conversation unless your client invites it.

- Avoid asking your client very direct questions. Clients find very direct questions rather embarrassing and even slightly impertinent. Where you do want an answer to a very specific and (for you) important question, find a way to express it in a more subtle form of words. For example, rather than saying, 'Do you want to employ me as a consultant along the lines of the proposal that I sent to you last week?', say, 'Were any of the ideas in the proposal that I sent to you last week of interest to you?'

- Avoid the hard sell at all costs. You are a consultant, not an insurance salesman. Nothing is more likely to put a client off than a barrage of 'hard sell' verbiage emphasising how clever you are, how much expertise you have, and how inexpensive you are compared with your competitors. You simply cannot say such things. There is no need to be pompous about it, but you must certainly give your clients the impression that you are no more privileged to be working with *them* than they are privileged to be working with *you*. Besides, you can never work productively with a client unless you both feel you are working on equal terms, anyway, and if you think about it, the hard sell – for all its bluster – is really a form of grovelling. Don't grovel, but be professional.

- Never, *never*, refer to anything negative about your consultancy.

126
- Never criticise a rival consultancy. This always sounds most unprofessional.

If you are receiving the telephone call and are not expecting it, you will have to plan the conversation as you talk rather than beforehand. All the same, the above rules still apply. And make sure, before you say your goodbyes, that you know how to spell the name of the client organisation and the name of the person to whom you have just been talking. *Never* assume that you know how to spell a name merely from the sound. English is one of the most unphonetic languages in the world and although we learn as children to read by recognising words as patterns which have meaning rather than as groups of letters which we read individually, the accurate spelling of proper names remains a problem all our lives. Even a very common and, on the face of it, easy to spell name such as 'John Smith' can be spelt as 'Jon Smith', 'John Smyth', 'Jon Smyth', 'John Smythe' and 'Jon Smythe'. As for names of client organisations, making a guess at spelling a name can leave you spelling it with wild inaccuracy.

Why do I place this emphasis on the spelling of names? The reason is very simple, and here I come to the first of the two precepts which you will find in Dale Carnegie's *How to Win Friends and Influence People.*

Carnegie's book is unquestionably one of the great instructional books of all time, to say nothing of being by far the best 'how to' title. One of the few 'how to' books which actually delivers what it promises, this book is a masterly set of observations on how paying heed to certain aspects of practical human psychology can help you get ahead in life and in business. In many ways the book is a kind of bible for post-war capitalism, and although its assumption that getting ahead in business is mainly a matter of putting these observations into practice (Dale Carnegie is particularly fond of quoting instructive anecdotes featuring his namesake the great capitalist and philanthropist Andrew Carnegie) seems a little naive to us nowadays, you will get a great deal from Carnegie's book; so read it. And if you have already read it, read it again, for you would do well to keep much of its advice in the forefront of your mind when you set out on your great task of starting your own high-income consultancy.

127

In addition to Paul Hawken's *Growing a Business, How To Win Friends and Influence People* is the only instructional book – apart from this one – which I recommend you read before you start your own consultancy.

Back to the first of the two Dale Carnegie principles which I think are of particular importance to a consultant who wants his client to think that he is wonderful. The first precept here is: *The most important sound in the world to any person is the sound of their name.*

I cannot prove the validity of this precept to you by any scientific means, but the precept is profoundly true, all the same. It follows that the *spelling* of someone's name is also of immense importance, and since you will need to write to your client at some point, it is very much in your interests to check up on spellings when you are talking to the client. Ultimately, the name of the client's organisation will not be as important to them as their own name, but it will have considerable importance, none the less, and you do not want to misspell it any more than you wish to misspell the personal name of your client contact.

Another thorny problem which you will have to deal with when initiating telephone calls to prospective clients is what to do if the person you are trying to speak to is not in.

My advice on this matter is firm and clear: by all means mention to the person who takes your call who you are and why you telephoned, *but if this is the first time that you are telephoning your client contact, do not expect him to return your call but instead call him again yourself.*

When you are basically trying to sell something (and if you are contacting a prospective client what you are trying to sell are your services as a consultant) it is simply not courteous to leave a message asking somebody to call you back. Besides, you will want to control your timing of how you approach the prospective client, and if you ask to be called back you will have put the timing into your prospect's hands.

Where your prospective client is someone whom you have already met – for example if you have visited them in their offices and sent them a proposal and now want to find out whether the proposal is of interest to them – you have to be careful about seeming too eager to win the business. Many prospective clients will feel that they are superior to you because it is you who are trying to sell *them* something, and they will be only too ready to construe eagerness as desperation. I suggest you only make two phone calls to their office, leaving a message each time, and then wait for them to call you back. If they don't call you back within a week or so, it may be that they are not really interested in working with you anyway, but since in this case you would have nothing to lose, I would call them again in a week or so anyway (this time making sure that you do talk to them) so that you can find out what the position really is.

LETTERS

If professionalism on the telephone is a prerequisite for the initial stages of a relationship with a client, it is equally essential that the letters you write are also marked by a high degree of professionalism from the outset.

You have already read about my recommendations for having your own stationery on which to write letters. Good, professional stationery is a starting point, but it is only a starting point, for what matters now is what you actually type onto the stationery.

And you will, of course, need to type it. There is certainly room for handwritten letters in the consultancy business; a brief, informal letter to a long-term client contact can sometimes be very effective if handwritten, but the letters which you write to prospective clients are going to need to be typewritten, ideally by a computer printer rather than by a typewriter. A computer printer will always give a more professional finished look to the letter than a typewriter can.

In the next chapter, which deals with the matter of winning new business, I give an example of the type of new business letter which you could write to a client. Here, what matters is to point out the various standards to which your letters *must* adhere:

■ There must be no spelling mistakes. Anyone who sends out a letter with a spelling mistake because they cannot be bothered to check the spelling of a difficult word has no right to call himself professional. Many computer word processing packages contain spellcheck functions, but you cannot always rely on these, as they do not normally contain proper names or much in the way of a technical vocabulary. In particular, it is absolutely fatal to misspell the name of the person to whom you are writing, and the name and address of his organisation.

■ There must be no 'typos'. These are not spelling mistakes, but errors in the typing. If you use a computer printer it

129

should be possible to avoid typos completely by paying careful attention to the letter on the screen before you print it out. Be particularly careful with the words 'of' and 'or', and 'if' and 'it'. On a QWERTY keyboard the 'r' is immediately above the 'f' so it is easy to confuse the two . The letters 't' and 'f' present similar problems. And if you mix these words up, the fact that they are very common words and your eyes usually only skim-read them makes errors here very difficult to spot.

Generally, until you get the hang of sending out letters with no typos in them you would do well to ask somebody else to read through a letter on the screen in case you have inadvertently included any typos which you yourself are unable to spot. For some reason, it is always more difficult to spot typos in a document that you have written yourself rather than in a document that someone else has written.

130

- The letter should be written on your letterhead, and should have the name and address of the person to whom you are writing on the left and starting about an inch under the text at the top of the letterhead. Below the name and address put the date, writing the date out in full, e.g. 29 August 1993 rather than 29/8/93 which always looks terribly unfriendly. A couple of inches below the date write the salutation, e.g. 'Dear Mr Smith'.

- Even in a completely cold new business mailing, always write to a named contact, never to a job title. I come back to this point again in the next chapter, but it is important to set it down here.

- Do not include the forename of the person to whom you are writing in the salutation unless you have *either spoken to them on the telephone at some length or else met them at least once*. In North America and Britain, the business world is becoming increasingly informal, and forenames are used soon after a business acquaintance begins, but using someone's forename when you are writing to them for the first time and when you have never met them or spoken to them on the telephone in an other than cursory manner is stretching informality dangerously close to impertinence.

When writing to women, use the increasingly acceptable 'Ms' in the first instance. One big advantage of 'Ms' is that it avoids the embarrassing necessity of finding out whether or not it is 'Mrs Smith' or 'Miss Smith'. Of course, if you have met the woman in question and talked in some detail, you can feel free to address her in the letter by her forename.

- Keep initial letters business-like and to the point. There simply is no room in them for silliness, frivolity or anything in the least self-deprecating.

- Keep initial letters to one page in length, *at all costs*. You cannot expect someone to whom you are writing for the first time to read more than one page. By the way, bear in mind that if the letter doesn't grab that person right from the start, he may not even bother to read that first page in its entirety.

Finally, remember when making an initial contact with a client that *from the first moment when your prospective client hears about (or is told about) your existence you are in effect on trial by the client, with the client assessing you as a reliable business contact and (possibly) consultant worth hiring from the very beginning.*

In many ways this process of being on show to your prospective client from the very first moment is analogous to being involved in a courtship. In the long run it may be an almost equally important part of your life as any long-term relationship.

As in a courtship, you will want, in the initial stages, to be on your very best behaviour with your prospective client. You will want to show the very best aspects of yourself to the client, too. Time enough, when you have got to know the client really well and have shown what you can do for them, for them to realise that, whatever your plus points, you are only human, after all.

STARTING A HIGH-INCOME CONSULTANCY

Step 2: starting to get professionally involved with clients

The two most fundamental aspects of good client relations when you start to get professionally involved with clients are: (1) knowing how to arrange meetings and how to conduct yourself at meetings; and (2) writing proposals and reports for clients.

Of course, these two aspects of your activity are also very important for when you are working with clients on an ongoing basis, but they are particularly crucial to your success at getting those ongoing client relationships established. As such my discussion of this second step focuses on this.

132 ARRANGING MEETINGS AND CONDUCTING YOURSELF AT MEETINGS

Here is my ten-point guide to success when arranging and attending meetings.

1 Always write down the precise date, time and location of meetings in your diary *as soon as they are arranged*. Do not delay doing this; it is horribly easy to forget about a meeting – particularly if you are arranging several in conjunction with a new business campaign in the early days of your new SFC. Obviously, failing to turn up for a meeting because you have forgotten about it is disastrous, but it is hardly much better to have to telephone the organisation with whom you are meeting in order to check up on the precise time and location. If you do this, they will conclude (rightly) that you are anything but professional. If you can't remember the timing and location of a meeting, how can you remember the more complex details of any project which they may ask you to handle?

2 When you write down the date, time and location of a meeting in your diary, *always write down the client's telephone number next to the details of the meeting*. You will need this number if you are on your way to the client and get lost, or if you have been inadvertently delayed and want to warn them that you will be a little late.

3 Unless *absolutely unavoidable*, do not change the timing of a meeting your end. Doing this always looks unprofessional and silly. Of course, your client may change the timing, and you will just have to put up with that.

4 *Your personal appearance is extremely important when attending a meeting with a client, and particularly an initial meeting with a prospective client.* You *must* dress as smartly as you can. If you are a man, the crucial things to watch for are that your suit is well-pressed, that your tie matches and your shirt is buttoned up at the top, and that your shoes are well-polished. If you are a woman, aim to be equally stylish. I have already mentioned to you that when people hire consultants, they usually do so in the first instance to boost their own ego rather than because the problem which they are hoping you, the consultant, will solve is oppressing them. Even if it *is* oppressing them, they will still hire you basically for reasons of ego-boost.

133

This explains why your personal appearance is so important at the initial meeting and at successive meetings. In business, people want to do business with other people who they perceive to be successful. As Mark McCormack states very succinctly in *What They Don't Teach You at Harvard Business School,* 'people want to do business with winners.' So you have to look like a winner from the outset. Of course, ultimately what is going to matter to your clients is the quality of your thoughts and the way you express those thoughts in words and in writing, but if you don't look the part from the outset, you aren't going to have a chance to show your clients what a good brain you have, because they won't hire you.

Remember, too, that personal hygiene is also a function of personal appearance. Always use a deodorant and bear in mind that you might need to use it again during the day in the summer. Be careful about oral hygiene, too. It is a good idea to take your toothbrush and toothpaste along with you in your briefcase and to brush your teeth after lunch even if you did not dine at the New Madras Extra-Hot Curry House.

5 Do not be late for a meeting unless an unavoidable emergency has occurred. When you attend a meeting with a prospective client, you are in effect trying to sell something (i.e. your services) and good salespeople are never, *ever*, late. If you have never visited the client's premises before, give yourself plenty of time to find where you are going. Indeed, it is always a good idea to aim to arrive 15 minutes or so early for a meeting. You may want to freshen up before the meeting, but even if you don't, the receptionist will not object to you sitting in reception until it is time for the meeting.

6 When you meet the prospective client for the first time, give them a warm smile and shake hands. The first visual image that they have of you is important, so make sure that it will be a positive one.

7 When inside the meeting room, do not put your brief-case on a chair or table, but *on the floor*.

8 You *must* know exactly what you are seeking to get from the meeting *before* you go into the meeting.

Essentially, all meetings between a consultant and a prospective or existing client take place in order to discuss an aspect of the client's activities with which the consultant hopes to assist the client. This being the case, what you should be aiming to achieve at the meeting is *either* to obtain sufficient information about that aspect of the client's activities for you to be able to go away and prepare a proposal for a definite course of action which you would like to undertake on the client's behalf and for which you will be paid, *or* to obtain definite agreement from the client, there and then at the meeting, for you to go away and undertake that action; given that you will, of course, need to get from the client a signed agreement relating to the activity *prior* to starting it.

You cannot always know in advance of a meeting which of these two possible outcomes is likely to occur, but do your utmost to steer the meeting in one of these two directions, *given that you must, as with your initial telephone conversations, avoid the hard sell*.

9 Make sure that you take any relevant documentation to the meeting. This would include business cards (these are essential), any of your corporate literature, any visual aids such as flip-charts and overhead projector foils, and – something that I have always found very useful – a file which contains numerous clear plastic jackets in which you can place examples of work already completed, flattering letters which clients have written to you about the excellence of your services, and other items. If, as a completely new start-up, you have no such documentation to show off from your time as a consultant, there is no reason why you should not include material from your former time as a salaried employee, given that what you are including has some relevance to the activity which you are proposing to undertake on the client's behalf.

10 The key to attending meetings as a consultant is to *listen*. After all, the reason why you are there in the first place is, presumably, because your client has a problem (whether temporary or ongoing) and needs your help. How can you be of assistance to the prospective client if you do not know what the problem is?

On the other hand, you cannot necessarily leave it to the client to *say the first thing* at the meeting. After all, if you have written a new business letter to the client you will presumably have requested a meeting at the end of the letter. Even if the client has requested to see you as the result, say, of having heard about you from one of his business contacts, he may still basically prefer you to kick off the meeting. Another factor is that clients are sometimes rather in awe of consultants, even a little frightened of them. So it may be up to you to break the ice.

The way to do this is not to fire a couple of party poppers at the ceiling but instead to introduce yourself *briefly* and summarise your previous experience and the areas of activity that your consultancy will cover. *Then*, if you already know what problem the client has, ask them to tell you about it. Otherwise, tell the client that you would be very interested to know what they are currently doing in terms of whatever specialisation you are offering as a consultant. Let the conversation develop from there, but above all, *listen*.

WRITING PROPOSALS AND REPORTS

A great deal of nonsense is spoken about writing proposals and other kinds of report. Although there are certainly some things which can be usefully borne in mind by anybody who wants to be an effective writer (if you've forgotten what I said on this score, turn back to page 30), the fact remains that no one can teach you how to write well.

On the other hand, you do not need to be another Ernest Hemingway or Charles Dickens to write a good proposal or report. Anybody who is able to string together an effective, coherent business letter should have no problems at all in writing well enough to produce a professional report.

136

What you should above all remember when writing reports is that your first and foremost task is to communicate information. It follows that anything which gets in the way of this information-communication process must be rigorously identified and removed, and anything which helps the information-communication process must be encouraged.

In terms of *how* you write, this means that you must choose words that fit in with the guidelines which I referred to on page 31: such as, when you write you should use shorter words rather than longer words, and you should also strive for conciseness and brevity of expression rather than unnecessary length and complexity. Beyond that, you are very much on your own when it comes to your writing style, but if you want to improve that style, practise your business writing whenever you can and read books written by people who know how to write. Try to assimilate some elements of their own style in your style. Paul Hawken's *Growing a Business* would be a good start, and since I have mentioned Hemingway you might like to read his novel *The Sun Also Rises*, a masterpiece of style which, apart from its story, should teach you something about how to use words to describe both concrete and abstract things in an interesting manner while keeping strict control over the words themselves and avoiding any hint of flowery prose or 'purple' writing.

Apart from taking steps to improve your writing style, you should also bear in mind the following guidelines:

- Give the report a title page by putting the report's title in the middle of a blank page and by putting your consultancy's name on the bottom left, as in Figure 5.1.

- Use a paragraph numbering system where you give each main section of the report a number (starting with 1) and give each sub-section within the main sections a number such as 1.1, 1.2, 1.3 and so on. This way, each paragraph receives a number depending on where it stands in the hierarchy of the main section, sub-section and any further groupings. So, for example, paragraph 2.3.1 means the first paragraph in the third sub-section of section two.

  The reason for using this system is that it will help to clarify your thoughts about how you should structure your report. It will also, amazingly, reduce what may seem a very daunting task to one that is readily manageable.

- Structure the report so that it starts by stating very clearly the problem that the client organisation is suffering. The report should then go on to say (briefly) something about your own organisation before you go on to the main part of the report, which should explain what you think the client organisation needs to do.

  Finish the report with a brief conclusion in which you summarise everything that you say in the report.

- Do your utmost to prevent there being any spelling mistakes or typos in the finished report.

- If you are going to give copies of your finished report to various members of staff who work for your prospective client, get the copies of the report professionally bound before handing them over.

137

If you are making a presentation to the client, in which you present the main recommendations of the report verbally and then hand over the copies of the report, *do not hand over the copies of the report until the presentation is over*. That way, your clients will concentrate on what you have to say to them, rather than concentrating on the copies of the report that are on the table in front of them.

Step 3: working with clients on an ongoing basis

Managing the ongoing relationship with a client in the most effective way is beyond doubt the real essence of how to make your clients think that you're wonderful. The initial stages of the client relationship should result in the client being already impressed by your professionalism. Now you have to build on that image by continuing to be seen as professional, while also ensuring that you are seen to be paying devoted attention to your client's needs and to being willing to spare no effort on your client's behalf.

As with other areas which are discussed in this book, it is not possible, in the final analysis, for me or anyone else to teach you how to work devotedly and professionally on behalf of your clients. Ultimately the level of service which you, the consultant, provide is a function both of your inherent skill and expertise and also of your *willingness* to spare no effort on behalf of your clients. However, by keeping the following guidelines in the front of your mind, you should maximise your own potential for making your clients think that you're wonderful when working for them on an ongoing basis.

1 *Cultivate a sincere interest in and empathy for those business problems which your clients have that relate to the specialisation which you are offering as a consultant.*

This is the most important guideline of all to making your clients think that you're wonderful on an ongoing basis, because ultimately you will only be able to achieve this if your

Figure 5.1   Example of a report title page

MARKETING PLAN FOR SMITH ASSOCIATES INCORPORATED

Prepared by:

James Essinger Associates
4 Ivy Place
York Road
Canterbury

Tel: 0227 472874

interest and empathy for your clients' business is *sincere*. You may briefly be able to fake such an interest and empathy, but such fakery will not last long.

Cultivate a genuine interest in and empathy for your clients' business problems by reminding yourself that if you can solve your clients' business problems, those problems will make you rich.

Besides, if you have followed the advice that I gave you earlier in this book and embarked on being a consultant in a specialisation that you already love, you should not find it necessary to fake an interest in those business problems which your clients have and which relate to your own specialisation.

2 *Resolve to spare no effort to assist your clients and to help them.*

This precept is simple, powerful and essential. You must spare no effort on your clients' behalf, even if this means sitting up until 3 a.m. in order to finish a report which your client wants to have on his desk the following morning. But if you *did* sit up until 3 a.m., there is no harm in discreetly mentioning this fact to your client.

3 *Ensure that your hard work is visible to your clients.*

Only religious martyrs or persons of an excessively self-deprecating temperament like hiding their light under a bushel, and as you are a consultant or are thinking of becoming a consultant, I hope I can assume that you are not too keen on either religious martyrdom or excessive self-deprecation.

The point is that if you want your clients to think that you're wonderful you *must* take every step to ensure that your hard work is seen by your clients. There is no room in the consultancy business for modesty, false or otherwise.

Which does not mean that you have to draw attention to your hard work in a flagrant and crudely boastful or conceited way. What you should do instead is recognise that there are three principal means by which your hard work will be visible to your clients, and never miss an opportunity to project yourself to the client by these means.

Firstly: you can telephone your client. Make sure that you talk to your clients regularly on the telephone in order both to let them know what you are doing for them and also to find out what new problems/challenges/difficulties they are facing. In fact, such telephone conversations will often produce important new business leads for you, but remember that the reason for the phone calls is not inherently to win new business, *but to communicate to the client what you are doing for them and to show the client that you are profoundly interested in their business.*

If you are not talking to your client on the telephone at least twice a week during the period while you are working for them on either an ad hoc or retainer basis, you are speaking to them too infrequently. Of course, you *must* have something to tell the client or ask them about; it is not enough to phone them 'for a chat', unless you know them very well indeed and know that they would appreciate this.

141

If you telephone your client and his or her secretary says that he is too busy to take the call right now, say that you will call back when he is less busy and do call back. If you leave the ball in the client's court by leaving a message the client may not call you back in the near future, and your relationship will in some way be blocked.

You should, I need hardly add, have ensured that your client is paying for all your telephone calls by arranging a deal which includes a charge for telephone expenses that will pay for your regular telephone contact and for other telephone calls that you need to make in the course of your work for the client.

Secondly: you can write letters and reports about your activity and send them to your clients. These are particularly important as they form a permanent record of your activity as a consultant. Unlike telephone calls, letters and documents can almost certainly be filed by your client.

I recommend that for all your clients you get into the habit of producing a monthly 'activity report' which lists in numbered summary form what you have done for your client during the month that is just coming to an end. Activity reports are equally important for ad hoc or retainer accounts, except that with ad hoc accounts you may need to consider preparing your activity reports on a more regular basis than once a month if the project is particularly time-intensive. You should, of course, also write an activity report when the ad hoc project has come to an end.

Remember, incidentally, that ad hoc clients need to be kept as happy as retainer clients. The ad hoc client of today may become the retainer client of tomorrow.

Thirdly: you can tell your client what you are doing for them during a meeting. For retainer clients, you should be meeting them face to face *at least* once a month. For ad hoc clients, how often you meet them will again depend on how work-intensive the project is, but unless it is a very short project (requiring, say, less than six days of your time) I recommend that you meet the client to discuss progress (and to find out whether there is anything that they feel you are *not* doing which you ought to be doing) in the middle of the project as well as at the beginning and at the end.

4 *Cultivate a habit of giving your client sincere flattery as and when it seems appropriate.*

This is the second precept in this book that I am lifting from Dale Carnegie's *How To Win Friends and Influence People.*

Apart from the basic human needs of shelter, food and sexual fulfilment, people want to feel good about themselves. Often, of course, they don't, but since you are being hired by your client to act as a consultant, you should not miss a chance of proffering sincere flattery to your client. Such sincere flattery will, if it is properly done, endear yourself to your client and help him to think that you're wonderful.

The key word here is *sincere.* Your flattery has got to be sincere

142

or it will seem absurd and even outrageous.

The best way to offer sincere flattery is to keep your flattery discreet and subtle. You *can* praise a client's astuteness in having been able to win a particular piece of business, but you must confine the flattery to matters relating to the client's professional life.

5 When you make an assessment of or judge an aspect of your client's activity, make sure that your assessment or judgement is constructive.

Anybody can criticise, but only people who are thoughtful can criticise constructively, which basically means that you make positive suggestions to improve whatever is the subject of criticism. Remember that the very word 'criticism' has become used to denote negative criticism, whereas the word's original meaning denoted a much more neutral, even constructive, process. Try – in your own thinking and behaviour – to return the word to its original meaning. Indeed, it is useful to recall that as a consultant you are not there to offer criticism but rather a *critique*: the word 'critique' does not have the same negative connotations as 'criticise' or 'criticism' and is a better word for you to have in your mind when you think about what you are seeking to do as a consultant, since the word implies constructive criticism.

143

6 Get into the habit of thinking before you speak.

Remember that, when you are running a consultancy, what you and your fellow consultants (if any) are basically being paid for is the quality of your thought.

This being the case, you, the consultant, *must* do your utmost to be regarded by your client as a thoughtful, perceptive person. Which means that you must *never* give snap judgements to your client; whether over the telephone or in a meeting. Always give yourself time – even if it is only a few minutes – to deliberate the matter before you give your judgement.

For example, say you have a client whose organisation has

always been known as Albion Lingerie Limited, and your client gets it into his head that giving the organisation a fruitier name will improve sales. So the client phones you up, and asks your opinion of the proposed new name: Naughty Knickers Limited. You, most likely, will feel that this is a dreadful name, but *don't* say that right away. Instead, *say you would like some time to think the matter over and tell the client you would like to call him back in half an hour or so.*

Then, when you call the client back half an hour later, give a *reasoned response* to his suggestion. If you don't like the suggestion, say why. On the other hand, if during the half hour you have reflected that while the new name sounds pretty sleazy, it may help to drum up sales in the marketplace where your client operates, say so. In either case, even if ultimately your client does not act on your advice, he will respect you for having taken the trouble to think the matter through. And if you do not like the name that he suggested, try to think of a better name, if you can. Remember the need to offer constructive criticism.

144

You should adopt the same policy in a meeting. Try to give yourself time to have a good think about the matter. Even if you are in a meeting where you have little choice but to give a rapid response to a question, *sit in silence for half a minute or so and think about it.* You have no idea how effective it can be in a corporate meeting for a consultant to sit there, thinking.

7 Remember that as a consultant you should above all be playing a pro-active role in your clients' professional lives, and in particular you should get into the habit of initiating ideas which will assist your clients.

This guideline should be self-explanatory, although this does not make it any less important. As a consultant, you should always try to generate ideas and suggestions for activity rather than simply sitting back and being a sounding-board for your clients' own ideas.

8 *Understand that people hire consultants to boost their own egos, so don't be afraid of being a little demanding.*

I have already, earlier in this book, referred to one of the psychological reasons why people hire consultants – to boost their own egos – so bear this in mind and don't be afraid of being a little *demanding*, whether in terms of the fee that you are charging your client, or in terms of how you expect to be treated by your client (or his secretary). If you are a little demanding, what your client will think, in effect, is 'this fellow is a demanding person because he is talented and has abundant expertise. What a clever chap I am to have hired him!'

Of course, you cannot be too demanding, because that would be impertinent, and you will, in the end, have to deliver the goods in terms of what you do for the client if the client is to retain this high opinion of you. However, you are a consultant, and if you have been kept waiting for 20 minutes for a meeting which your client requested, you are entitled to an apology. And if your client's secretary is rude to you or stroppy over the telephone without any cause, you are entitled to raise the matter discreetly with your client. Give yourself a high status, and your client will tend to believe that you deserve a high status.

145

9 *Try to surround yourself with an aura of expertise.*

Ultimately, you have to make your clients feel that your opinion is worth soliciting and that you are a person who is brimful with expertise.

You can only make your clients believe this of you by doing things for them, and making suggestions, which impress them, but even before achieving this you yourself need to believe that you are a person who is surrounded by an aura of expertise. If you believe this yourself (given that you have good reasons for believing this) there is a much better chance that your clients will believe it, too.

6

Winning new business

Introduction

If money is the life-blood of the self-fuelling consultancy, new business is its skeleton. Your ability to generate new business for your SFC is ultimately going to decide whether your SFC has a long and prosperous future ahead of it, or is merely destined to collapse with a whimper.

There are three principal ways of winning new business for your SFC, and it is important, for the clarity of the discussion which follows, to distinguish clearly between them.

The primary method of winning new business

The most important way of winning new business – which I refer to here as the primary method – is where you win the business due to a referral: that is, because your name or your SFC's name has been given by one of your existing clients or business contacts to a third party who contacts you on an unsolicited basis. I also include within this method any additional business which you are able to win from your *existing* clients.

There can be no doubt that by far the largest proportion of new business won by consultancies stems from this method of referral, or additional business coming from an existing client. This is what we would expect, since consultancy services are, after all, supplied to people by people, and if the consultant and his client get on and work together fruitfully, the time will surely come when a client will want to sing the praises of his consultant, and it is precisely when this desire comes over the client that he is most likely to give a third party the information that leads to a referral.

How can you increase the level of referral business which you receive?

The first way is to *work hard, effectively and sincerely on behalf of your existing clients*. In business, as in other areas of human activity, word soon gets around if someone is very good at what they do.

The second way – and do not neglect this – is to widen your profile and enhance your reputation in your particular professional or industrial sector by means of projecting yourself as an authority and expert in your own sector.

There are various ways of doing this.

147

Firstly, you can offer to speak at relevant professional or industrial seminars, where you will regard your recompense for the time and trouble taken over the writing and presentation of your speech as being not the nominal, or in fact possibly non-existent, fee that you receive for doing this, but rather the exposure which you get to potential clients, or to people who influence the decisions of potential clients.

Secondly, you can write articles under your own name for relevant professional or industrial journals.

Thirdly, you can write books on subjects related to your profession or industry.

Fourthly, you can start and edit a newsletter for your profession or industrial sector. Not only can the writing of a newsletter and the selling of newsletter subscriptions be a superb way of widening your reputation and broadening your profile, the newsletter can also be a very useful profit centre itself. However, you have got to like writing newsletters, if you want to do this, and there is a distinct danger that you might find yourself spending time on the newsletter when you could be working for your clients, although this latter danger can be reduced by the simple expedient of only bringing your newsletter out, say, five or six times a year.

The secondary method of winning new business

The secondary method of winning new business is to make approaches to prospective clients with whom you have not yet worked. Although this method always has an inevitable air of 'hit and miss' about it, it can none the less be a very effective method of winning new business, but it needs to be handled properly.

In almost all cases, your first approach to prospective new clients in this way should be by letter. The only exception is where an existing client or other contact has given you the name of a prospective client who may be interested in your services and who has asked you to call them. In this case you would want to call them in the first instance, and you may be able to set up a meeting with them on the basis of the telephone call alone. Such a prospect as this is not exactly a referral, but neither is it a completely cold approach, either.

Otherwise, you should write a letter to your new business prospect.

The purpose of this letter is to get a meeting with the prospective client which will give you a chance to tell them, in a professional and modest way, what exactly you have to offer them and how you can help them. If you do your background work properly, the response rate to such letters can sometimes be surprisingly high, but that is indeed the proviso: *if you do your background work properly*. This, then, is what you need to do, step-by-step.

148

WRITING TO PROSPECTIVE CLIENTS

Step one

Begin by accepting that *you ought to send a batch of new business letters to prospective clients every week as a regular and important part of your SFC's activity.* You ought to do this even if you are up to your eyes in business already (it does happen) and cannot imagine how you are ever going to find a spare minute to work on any new business.

Sending out new business letters regularly is not only important for the general health of your SFC, it is also good for your morale as a consultant to come into regular contact with new business prospects, even if they do not need your services at present. Many prospective clients like to hear about what a consultant can offer them and like to keep the consultant's details on file. The new business activity that you undertake this week may not bear fruit in terms of fee-paying work for six months or longer, but having the prospect of that work in the future is very important if you are planning – as I hope by now you are – for your SFC to be the mainstay of your income for the rest of your working life.

149

Step two

Next, *do your basic research.* Basic research is absolutely essential to the success of any new business mailing. Essentially, what you have to do is to identify organisations that are likely to be users of your services. The sources of this information will depend on your particular specialisation, and may include one or more of the following:

- business pages of your telephone directory ('Yellow Pages' in the United States or the United Kingdom);
- lists of members of professional associations;
- lists of conference delegates. These are often available to people who attend a specific conference, although this is rarely in fact a cost-effective way of obtaining these lists, as

the cost of attending a conference can be very high. However, sometimes you can do a deal with a conference organiser, whereby – for example – you supply them with names and addresses of potential conference delegates in exchange for your receiving, in due course, details of all those who attended the event;

■ lists of exhibitors at exhibitions;

■ lists of visitors to exhibitions;

■ names of organisations which advertise in your respective trade publication (many consultants overlook this source of possible new business contacts, but it is an important one, if only because such advertisers have already demonstrated, by buying the advertisement, that they believe in laying out some money for the chance of making their business more successful and profitable);

■ names of organisations which you read about in the editorial pages of your trade press or in general business publications such as the *Wall Street Journal* or the *Financial Times*. Do bear in mind, though, that you may not be the only consultant who is writing to organisations whose problems and/or objectives have been revealed in the media.

I must admit that in my own work as a consultant I have always found lists of members of professional associations to be the best lists for my new business mailings. These lists are usually available at a very reasonable cost from the professional association, whereas lists of conference delegates or lists of exhibitors at exhibitions or lists of visitors to exhibitions are likely to be expensive or difficult to obtain. However, you should not necessarily be guided by my own experience, as it may be that for you another area of research will be the most fruitful.

What you should aim to be doing from this basic research is to *gather the names and addresses of at least 100 organisations which might be interested in using your services.* When you have done that, you are ready for the next step.

Step three

Write to these organisations, but *write to no more than about 15 organisations a week.*

I firmly believe that the key to successful business mailings is to write to a relatively small number of prospective clients a week, but to *keep up these mailings on a regular basis.*

The reason for this is twofold:

1 You *must* personalise each mailing, which means that unless you happen to know the name of the person at the organisation to whom you should be writing, you will need to telephone that organisation and find out from the receptionist who the person is. This takes time, and making your telephone calls and sending out only 15 letters which are all personalised is going to take you at least a morning. I do not think I can advise you to spend more than half a day per week on looking for new business by the secondary approach, because that will take away too much time from you which should be spent on working for your existing clients and thereby increasing the likelihood that you will obtain business through the primary method. The only exception to this is if business is currently very thin on the ground, in which case you may wish to spend more time on new business mailings.

2 Other things being equal, your new business mailings should be thoughtful and discreet rather than too wide-ranging. Remember that the people to whom you are writing are probably part of a small market or niche market, and they will talk to each other. If you fire new business letters off in all directions word will quickly get around that you are either: (a) desperate; or (b) unprofessional, and neither reputation is going to help you win new business.

The job title or role of the person to whom you should write at the prospective client organisation will depend both on the size of the organisation and the type of consultancy business in which you are in.

151

If you are writing to a small organisation (this is often something which you can ascertain when you make your phone call; indeed the organisation may tell you this themselves) you should write to the managing director.

If, on the other hand, you are writing to a larger organisation, you will have to write to whomever you imagine would be likely to be responsible for appointing you. This is something you will probably have to guess, as you cannot really expect the receptionist to tell you who appoints consultants in a particular field, because they are unlikely to know and besides, the organisation may never have appointed consultants before.

In any case, it should not be difficult for you to guess what the person's job title would be, and you can then call the organisation and ask for the name of the person who has that job title (but do remember not to assume, when you ask, that the person will necessarily be a man). If, for example, you are offering information technology services, you will probably need to write to the information technology director. If you are offering human resource consultancy, you will need to write to the personnel manager or the human resource manager (if there is one). If, on the other hand, you are offering public relations services, as I do, you should write to the marketing manager.

152

If, when you make your telephone call to find out the name of the person to whom you should be writing, you are asked why you want this information, tell the absolute truth – that you are a consultant working in such and such a field and you want to introduce yourself to the person in the organisation who is responsible for such and such a function. The vast majority of people, hearing such a request, will gladly give you the name of the relevant person, but on occasion you may be told either politely or not very politely that they have no need for your services. Fine, then thank them politely and replace the receiver. It's their loss, not yours. There is nothing to be ashamed of in wanting to sell your services. Even the President of America is a salesman: selling his policies to the American people both before and after he has been elected.

By the way, it sometimes happens that your exploratory telephone call to find out someone's name leads to you being able to introduce yourself over the telephone to a potential client. This may occur on occasions where you telephone a small organisation and wind up inadvertently talking to the boss and telling him about your services. If this happens, great, but remember that the purpose of your telephone call is not to sell yourself over the telephone (unless there is a very strong interest at the other end, I cannot recommend this course of action to any consultant) but simply to find out the name of the person to whom you should be writing.

Step four

Now write that letter. You write the letter on your letterhead and – as with other business letters – you include the name, organisation and address of the person to whom you are writing on the top left of the letter, starting below the bottom of the printed text at the top of your letterhead. Below this put the date, and then the salutation, which should be to 'Mr' somebody or 'Ms' somebody unless you already happen to know them.

153

Incidentally, if, while reading this book, you have been deliberating whether or not to buy a word processor, bear in mind that personalised new business letters are particularly easy to produce with a word processor, as once you have created the document that is your letter, all you need to do is change the name and address of the recipient and the salutation in order to create a new letter, which you can then print out. And once you have got the letter right and typo-free, you can be confident that the letter will have the same degree of perfection, no matter how many times you print it out.

I have already emphasised in the previous chapter the ultra-importance of avoiding any spelling mistakes in letters that you send out to your clients, and it should be obvious that letters sent to prospective clients are likely to be nothing more than a waste of a stamp, a letterhead and an envelope if they contain any typos or spelling mistakes. If they do, your prospective clients will assume that you are either unprofessional or in-competent, and rightly so.

As regards the actual text of the letter, this is so important an element of your success in winning new business – and there-fore to the overall success of your consultancy – that I ought to make some suggestions for how you compose your letters, even though basically your own text of new business letters is some-thing that you will have to work on yourself. The letter shown in Figure 6.1 is one that I have used with success to win new business.

I am not suggesting that your own new business letter should read anything like this, but you will probably find the various parts of this letter helpful when composing your own new business letters. In any event, here are my brief comments about the four paragraphs in the letter, with the paragraphs being referred to according to the letters at the end of them.

(A) I always find it a good idea to start a new business letter with a question. The question should be such that if the answer is, in effect, 'no', then the inference should be that your own consultancy will be able to undertake this service for the pros-pective client. Of course, the precise wording of the question that you ask at the start of your letter will depend on the *nature* of the consultancy service that you provide.

Not only is a question inherently interesting because it involves the reader in having to, in effect, formulate an answer, but a question like this has the huge advantage over a more pedestrian type of beginning (such as 'I am a consultant specialising in . . .' etc.) that it focuses on the needs of the recipient, not on your own needs.

(B) Here, you briefly introduce yourself and your consultancy and mention any specific experience which you or your con-sultancy has in terms of the particular market in which your recipient operates. This letter was directed to investment management organisations, so the relevant experience that I mention is appropriate for that sector.

154

Figure 6.1 Example of a new business letter

A. Prospect Esq.
General Investment Management Limited
100 Commercial Street
Anytown
AN1 2AA

Date

Dear Mr Prospect

Have you ever considered the great promotional advantages which your organisation could gain from a pro-active approach to obtaining editorial coverage in newspapers and investment industry journals read by your existing and potential clients? **(A)**

I am a writer and public relations consultant specialising in the international securities industry. I can reasonably claim to be an expert on investment management, having written the current *Euromoney Investment Management Training Manual*, as well as the recently published *The Investment Manager's Handbook.* **(B)**

In addition to writing under my own name, I also specialise in offering some organisations a service involving the drafting, clearing and distribution of press releases and the ghost-writing of full-length 'thoughtpiece' articles which appear in key financial media under my clients' byline. Coverage generated by this activity is an immensely powerful marketing tool for my clients; far more powerful than advertising could ever be. The cost of this service is quite modest; operating out of Canterbury I can pass my relatively low overheads on to my clients. My daily rate is just £250. **(C)**

I would greatly appreciate the opportunity to meet with you (on an entirely no-obligation basis, of course) in order to tell you more about this service and how it operates. If you are interested in meeting me, perhaps you could let me know. In the meantime, I am enclosing some biographical details, for your information. **(D)**

Thank you for your time over this matter. **(E)**

Kind regards

155

(C) Here, you detail the nature of the service that you are offering and how much it costs. If you believe that cost is one of your incremental advantages, don't be afraid to point this out, but do it in a discreet manner, as here.

(D) Here, you request a meeting. It is important to emphasise that this would be a no-obligation meeting. You can also include in this paragraph a brief explanation of any enclosures which you are sending.

(E) This is a pleasant and courteous way to end the letter, but don't put this in if it means that your letter will run to two pages. *You must confine your new business letter to one page.* You cannot expect a busy potential client to wade through an unsolicited letter which is longer than one page.

Step five

Finally, put the letter in an envelope. If you have a brochure which gives information about your SFC, you might like to include it in the mailing, although it isn't necessary and you may be better advised to wait until you reach the meeting stage before you give away your precious literature. After all, you must face the fact that at least two-thirds of the new business mailings that you send out will be put straight into the bin. That's how the business world works.

A useful alternative to including your brochure in the mailing is to compose a one-page biographical summary of your professional life to date and include it with the letter. This will establish your credentials without wasting expensive brochures. However, this approach is probably most effective where you are starting or running the consultancy yourself, since if there are several of you running it you will not be doing justice to what you have to offer if you only include your own biography, and including several biographies would look a little silly.

One final piece of advice about your new business mailing: *handwrite the details on the envelope.* I am convinced that handwritten envelopes are regarded with more attention and

156

interest by their recipients than typewritten or printer-written envelopes. Reflect on your own experience of receiving a mailing: don't you always pay more attention to handwritten envelopes?

True, the envelope may be opened by the recipient's secretary, in which case it won't matter much either way, but many executives nowadays prefer to open their own mail, and if your envelope is handwritten and not obviously a circular it is particularly likely that it will be opened by its recipient.

That said, *don't* write 'Private' or 'Private and Confidential' on the envelope. Nothing is more likely to annoy your recipient than for him to open what he imagines is a personal letter only to discover that it's a letter from someone trying to sell him consultancy services.

Step six 157

Wait and see what happens. Some consultancies like to follow up a new business mailing with a telephone call a week or so later to the prospective client. I have on occasion done this, but I have never found it to be effective. It seems basically pushy and unprofessional. If your prospective client is interested in meeting you, he will get back to you of his own volition. Remember what I said about the hard sell: that it is a form of grovelling.

Of course, if you *do* say in your letter that you will be following up the letter with a telephone call, then make sure that you make that call and make sure that the recipient of the letter knows that you have made the call. Otherwise, you might be perceived as breaking the very first undertaking that you have made to your potential client, and the potential client may be less than willing to become a proper client.

The tertiary method of winning new business

The tertiary method of winning new business is to use traditional techniques such as advertising and public relations to market yourself.

In many ways, the techniques that I mentioned above to enhance your reputation are all a form of public relations, but what I have in mind here are more formal marketing initiatives, such as would be involved if you launched an advertising campaign to get your consultancy's name in relevant professional or trade newspapers and journals, or if you retained a public relations consultancy to drum up editorial coverage for you in similar media.

I really cannot recommend that you use either advertising or public relations in any kind of formal sense until you are very well-established as a consultancy and can afford to shoulder the loss if the advertising and/or public relations campaign brings you nothing in terms of new business. Because, unfortunately, it is perfectly possible to spend a large sum on advertising or a public relations service and to wind up with no new business at all.

158

On the other hand, if your consultancy has been established for several years, and if you want your profession or industry to know more about your success, then a smallish advertisement in a journal or newspaper might be very useful for you.

Do not neglect the possibility of sponsorship, also. This does not only offer consultancies the chance to project themselves quite widely, but also sometimes results in you being invited to sports and social events connected with the sponsorship which may provide useful opportunities to entertain your clients.

New business meetings

In the previous chapter I discussed how to arrange meetings and to conduct yourself at them. When attending new business meetings you really are on show, and must strive from the outset to make a superb impression. There really is no room for anything less, if you want to work with the prospect on a long-term basis and for the prospect to become a client of your high-income consultancy.

As I explained in the previous chapter, one important objective of a meeting is for you to obtain sufficient information about a client's needs and problems for you to be able to go away and write a proposal for some activity by your consultancy on the client's behalf directed towards meeting those needs and solving those problems.

New business proposals

The better your new business proposal is, the deeper the understanding it shows of the client's needs and problems and the more effective your suggested solutions appear, the more likely you are to get the client's business. So before you start writing anything, have a really good think about how you can be of assistance to your prospective client.

159

In the previous chapter I suggested how to write a good proposal for activity, and everything I said then applies equally to new business proposals. The only additional comment that needs to be made here is that, while your proposal should display the depth of thought and height of resourcefulness that you have brought to bear on thinking about the client's problems, you *should be careful not to put very detailed proposals for specific activity in your proposal.*

What you ought rather to do is to talk generally of what you would be aiming to do and to hint at how you might do this without being too specific.

If you are too specific, your client might just decide to do everything you have recommended himself, or might give the proposal to an old friend of his who just happens to have set up as a consultant, and ask him to get on with it.

In either case you will probably receive a polite thank you for your efforts, but you will not receive a penny.

Remember that you are in business to make money for yourself. You must bear that objective in mind, and accept that your prospective clients may be perfectly willing to exploit your intelligence and expertise and not pay you a penny.

You mustn't let them get away with this, so don't be too specific when writing your new business proposals.

The new business dossier

Once you become experienced at winning new business, you may find it very useful to compile a regularly-updated new business dossier into which you write the names and contact details of organisations which are not yet your clients but which you would like to become your clients. You should also try to find out which consultancy (if any) the organisation is using at present, and keep this in the dossier along with the names and contact details of the potential client organisation itself.

Client agreements

Assuming that you have won your new business, what form should your written agreement with your client take?

I have emphasised earlier in this book the great importance of written agreements. By all means feel free to go to a lawyer and draw up a lengthy and long-winded client agreement if you must, but my advice is not to do that unless this really is a major piece of business which will require you to employ other people in order to service it and if you really would feel more secure with a detailed agreement full of legalese.

The disadvantages of such highly detailed agreements are: firstly, they can be quite expensive to draw up; second, they run the grave risk of damaging your (presumably) initially good relationship with the client by making yourself seem very tough and greedy; and third, long-winded agreements do *not* necessarily protect you against unforeseen eventualities any more than shorter and less formal agreements.

In any case, what is really going to determine the success, or otherwise, of your relationship with your client is the goodwill that exists between you. You can't somehow force the relationship by drawing up a complex and tough-looking agreement. All that will happen is that your client will get frightened by the agreement and send it off to his own legal department (which will probably be better equipped to produce tough agreements than you are), thereby causing delay in getting the agreement signed, the activity started, and the first payment in your pocket. Even worse, the client may refuse to sign your agreement at all.

Having said that, don't let me stop you drawing up a complex and long-winded agreement if you have set your heart on doing that. But if you want to avoid all the hassle and possible difficulty that goes with such an agreement, all you need to do is to write your client a letter in which you specify:

161

1 what you will be doing for them;
2 how many days of your consultancy time will be devoted to this activity. If it is an ad hoc project the letter should specify the total number of consultancy days that you will be devoting to the project. If it is a retainer project the letter should specify how many days of your consultancy time you will devote to the project per month, and for how many months;
3 the total cost of your consultancy time for the project (if an ad hoc project) or the monthly cost of your consultancy time (for a retainer project);
4 details of any expense charges that have been agreed;
5 when the payments will be invoiced and the credit terms on which the invoices will be sent;
6 any details of how the agreement can be terminated (but this is not really necessary, as an ad hoc project will be terminated naturally once the project is completed, while a retainer agreement will also be terminated naturally when the retainer period has expired);
7 any other matter which is material to the agreement.

Once you have written this letter, sign it and make a photocopy, which you should also sign, then send both the original and the copy to your client and ask him to sign and date the original and the copy if he agrees with the terms and to return the signed copy to you for your records.

Hey presto, you have an agreement signed with your client, and everything has been kept nice and friendly, with not a lawyer in sight.

There are two other connected areas, relating to winning new business, which ought to be mentioned before we pass onto the final chapter, which looks at expansion.

Presentations

The fact is that sooner or later you are going to have to make a new business presentation to a prospective client. A present-ation is a formal meeting where you use visual aids to present your consultancy's credentials and explain to the client what you could do for them.

Presentations are very popular in business. Most consultancies encounter the need to do a presentation at some point.

The points to remember about doing presentations are as follows:

- Everybody from your organisation who is present at the meeting should take part in the presentation. This is to maximise the impact in your client's mind of the team that will be looking after the client's business; although, as I mentioned earlier in this book, in many large consultancies new business teams do not actually work on the business when it is won.

- Presentations are really a form of performance art and *must* be rehearsed until they are near-flawless.

- Generally speaking, if a visual aid can go wrong, it will. Only use visual aids that you trust and know how to use. If in doubt, a simple flip-chart – which is basically like a large album with pages that you flip over – is easy to use and usually very effective.

- *Never* argue with your colleagues in front of a client, even in a friendly way.

- If anything goes embarrassingly wrong during a present-ation, don't draw attention to it but do your utmost to con-tinue undistracted. Sometimes a skilled presenter can turn an embarrassing mistake into a brief and amusing interlude which might even help the presentation along, but it is generally very risky to do this unless you know the client very well.

All the above guidelines also apply in informal meetings, as well as in presentations.

The final point to make about presentations is that you ought to question whether you really need to make a presentation in the first place. Often you don't. There is always something rather contrived and slightly pretentious about presentations, parti-cularly those connected with new business pitches. You will probably be much better off abandoning your plans for a presentation, and instead listening to the client tell you about his business needs and problems.

163

The trouble with most presentations for new business is that they have almost invariably been delivered in their entirety or in part to another prospective client, and this is usually only too clear to the client who is listening, particularly if – which has been known to happen – you confuse, during the presentation, the name of the client to whom you are now presenting with the name of the client to whom you presented the previous week.

All the same, I sometimes think that clients don't deserve much better than this, if they have asked you to take time over a presentation and yet asked several firms to pitch for the busi-ness, expecting each firm to spend time and money on a presentation.

The only case in which I can wholeheartedly recommend

presentations is where you are presenting the results of a report that you have been asked to prepare (for a fee) by your client. Here, there is clearly no competitive element and you can exploit to the full the opportunities which presentations give you to dramatise your findings and your thinking.

Taking part in competitive pitches

Finally, we come to the troublesome subject of competitive pitches, which I touched on just now.

In my five years of running my own consultancy, I have *never* accepted a request to take part in a competitive pitch. The reasons are simple: I believe that my consultancy offers clients the incremental advantages of specialisation within a niche market, a high degree of effort and expertise, and a very competitive fee. If that isn't enough for my prospective clients to confine their investigations of consultants to me alone, I'm not interested in working with them.

However, I am aware that I am not typical as a consultant, and in fact there are certain pieces of new business which it is almost impossible to win without having taken part in a competitive pitch. This is particularly true of consultancy work for very large corporations, and for government bodies (i.e. public sector).

All the same, a great deal of money and time can be wasted on competitive pitches, and when you are starting out as a consultant, time and money are among the most precious assets that you possess. So if you do decide to take part in competitive pitches, do your utmost to ascertain whether the prospective client is serious about the possibility of hiring your consultancy. If you get the impression that the client is not interested in this, think very seriously about whether you should spend considerable amounts of time, effort and money (whether because of real cost or opportunity cost) on the pitch.

164

7

Expansion

Introduction

First, let me be quite clear about what I mean by 'expansion'. I mean by this that you have started your SFC small, with only you or enough people working for your SFC to service the amount of business that you have at the outset. You can only hope to expand successfully if you are expanding from a position where you are running an efficient and professional consultancy, the size of which is strictly geared to the amount of business that you have. If you are running a 'pretend' consultancy that has surplus staff and resources from the outset, you will need to slim your consultancy down and make it properly proportionate to the amount of business that you have, before you can hope to expand successfully.

Expansion means taking on more staff. It may also mean moving, at some point, into larger premises, but for most consultancies it means increasing the number of staff.

Now, having been dogmatic throughout this book, I will cease being dogmatic.

I find it a reassuring thought that by the time you are ready to expand your SFC, you will be sufficiently experienced in running a successful consultancy for you no longer to need any advice which I may be able to give to you.

I find this thought a reassuring one because while I believe that there are certain reliable general guidelines which, if followed, will maximise the likelihood of you setting up and running a successful SFC, I am much less confident that such guidelines exist for determining when you should expand your consultancy.

Even more to the point, the question of whether, or *when*, you should expand your consultancy is so momentous a decision that I cannot possibly recommend that you take it on the basis of what you read in a book such as this. Instead, you should only take the decision after a full discussion of the matter with – at the minimum – your bank manager and your accountant and your colleagues. The reason for this is that the chances of getting things wrong are simply too high.

Having made this point, I would like to raise a few issues relating to the possible expansion of your SFC, as I feel that these issues may help to focus your thinking when you start considering whether to expand.

166

Do please bear in mind, however, that I am raising the following matters merely in order to let you see the kind of issues that you will need to face. They are not guidelines, and it would be irresponsible of me to pretend that they are.

The decision whether or not to expand

This decision is ultimately something that only you can reach, but it may be that the safest position to adopt is that you should only expand *if you have no alternative but to do so*.

There are two ways in which this might happen.

Firstly, you may be frequently finding yourself in a situation where you are meeting clients who are serious prospects but who are only likely to give you their business if they think you are more than a one-man band. This is a far cry from creating a 'pretend' consultancy. Instead, here it is the demand from the market that is pulling you to expand, which is precisely how it should be. If the self-fuelling consultancy is fuelling itself, then let it grow.

Secondly, you may have so much business from existing clients that you have no alternative but to take on additional staff to service it. You might naturally – and justifiably – be concerned that turning down the incremental work could jeopardise the existing relationship with the client. Similarly, if you have significantly more work than you can handle yourself, you may be in danger of spreading yourself too thinly, with the result that the quality of your consultancy's work is suffering. Recruiting fellow consultants and/or support staff provides an important 'comfort factor', so that you can hope to maintain the quality of your service, or, which may ultimately be equally important for the success of your consultancy business, enable you to take a *holiday*.

Having said this, there is no doubt that expansion raises a whole new set of questions and potential problems, not least of which is the possibility that you will before long have created around you the corporate hierarchy and political structures that you wanted to escape from by setting up an SFC. Other potential difficulties are the added responsibilities you will face in dealing with the welfare of others and in making good your financial commitments to them, and the fact that your existing clients may not want another face (often less experienced) working on their business, and if they get the new face, they may wind up not liking that person and being unwilling to go on using your consultancy's services.

167

The criterion which relates volume of business to number of staff

There is a consensus in the consultancy business that a new recruit should be able to look after business worth at least three times their salary. This figure is, however, only a guide.

So, for example, if you are taking on a new recruit at a salary of £20,000 per annum, that recruit would have to look after, on their own, at least £60,000 of business over the year in order to justify their salary.

Some consultancies regard this 'three times' factor as breaking down into:

- 40 per cent of the total amount of business worked on by the recruit to pay the recruit's salary;

- 40 per cent of the total amount of business worked on by the recruit as a contribution towards the consultancy's overheads;

- 20 per cent of the total amount of business worked on by the recruit to form the consultancy's profit. (You ought to bear in mind, by the way, that much or all of this could be cancelled in the recruit's first year due to recruitment agency and/or recruitment advertising costs.) Besides, it may well be that the recruit will only start being really profitable for you once he has worked with you for at least one year.

The need to have cash in the bank before you recruit

A general wisdom in the consultancy business is that you should not recruit somebody unless you have cash on deposit in the bank amounting to at least three months' worth of underlying costs for the consultancy, including the salaries of all staff (the new recruit included).

So, for example, if you are at present a one-man band and you are thinking of recruiting somebody, and if the consultancy will cost you £10,000 per month to run after you have taken on the new recruit – with this £10,000 to include your own monthly salary, your overheads and the monthly salary of the new recruit – you should have at least £30,000 cash in the bank before you take on your new recruit.

The need to recruit efficiently and cost-effectively

Many consultancies spend far too much money and effort on recruitment. The ease with which one can recruit good staff is, of course, to a large extent dependent on the condition of the economy. In the boom period of the mid-1980s, recruiting good people was always difficult. However, I am now writing (August 1993) in a latter end recessionary climate, when there are still more good people out there than jobs for them.

A small and discreet classified recruitment advertisement in your leading trade journal is much more likely to produce the result you want than hiring some hyped and overpriced recruitment agency who will be more concerned with getting a high fee from you than finding people who will really add something to your business. And since you will need to interview candidates anyway, you may as well focus on candidates who will not cost you a high proportion of their initial salary in fees if you take them on, as candidates who come through a recruitment agency will.

Sorry, I've become dogmatic again. I do apologise.

169

The need to recruit the right sort of person

Many consultancies get this wrong, and recruit people who are either too senior or too junior for what is required. Deciding what sort of person you want to recruit *before* you start the recruitment ball rolling is essential.

A good approach, to help you in your search for the most suitable candidate, is to write down, on one side of a piece of paper, the job description of what your ideal candidate would be like, and of what they would be capable.

Ideal recruits do not exist and not everyone will have all the necessary qualities. However, if too many of these qualities are missing from a given candidate, you should be aware of the danger of being tempted into placing too much emphasis on their charming personality.

Another useful practical test when considering a candidate for recruitment is to go through your own outstanding consultancy assignments and mentally tick off what the potential recruit could do for you. If only about half of the assignments look suitable for the candidate, then this person is probably not the correct person for you. You should also keep on 'profiling' the characteristics of the person you need so that you can try and identify them well in advance. For some exceptionally good candidates, persuading them to join you might take some time.

Finally, it is worth bearing in mind that you can always ask a candidate in whom you are interested to work with you for a few days on a trial basis so that you and the candidate can get some idea of how you work together. However, if you are doing this it only seems fair to pay the candidate for their time.

170 The need to guard against your recruits stealing your clients

Most consultants who have experience of recruiting staff agree that the danger of a new recruit getting so deeply involved with clients that he steals them – often using them to start up his own consultancy in the process – is very real.

The danger is usually reckoned as being greater when the recruit is a senior one, since a more junior recruit is less likely to get so deeply involved with clients. However, junior recruits can become senior staff with relative rapidity in the consultancy business, and there is also the simple fact that the better your recruit becomes at his job, the greater the danger that he will steal your clients.

Most consultancies try to solve this problem by requiring new recruits to sign a contract of employment in which they agree not to work for any of your clients for a certain period after terminating employment with you. The longer the period of abstention, the stricter the contract, but also the greater the risk that, if the contract was ever challenged in court, the court may decide that it regards the contract as an unreasonable restriction of the person's right to earn a living.

Generally speaking, one year is regarded as about the maximum time that a court will support you in your desire to keep what is yours, yours. Beyond that, the court may decide – not, perhaps, unreasonably – that if your own relationship with the client was so good, you would be able to continue to secure the client's business, having had a year in which to do so.

Final thoughts on expansion

Even here, in this chapter on expansion, remember that even after you have expanded, you must still keep open the option of contracting again if it seems like the best idea. When a consultancy contracts, this is not always a sign of failure, but often a sensible move. Too many consultants measure success in terms of increased turnover in successive years, rather than in terms of underlying profit trends. If a large contract ends abruptly, some kind of cutback may be required if the consultancy is going to have continued health and long-term viability. Managing contraction may not be as exciting as managing growth, but it can certainly be as financially rewarding.

171

When you are considering expansion, reach again – if you still have it – for the piece of paper on which you wrote down your motivations. Be honest and ask yourself whether expansion is a knee-jerk reaction to a sudden and perhaps temporary increase in your SFC's volume of business, or fundamental to where you want your SFC to be in five years' time.

If you *are* expanding, and doing better and better, sooner or later you will receive a financial offer for your SFC. You will need to assess the offer on its own merits or demerits, but do remember that you have the option – assuming by now that your SFC has been incorporated – of selling a controlling share in your SFC and still remaining at the helm of it. Remember that if you sell out completely, you may never again have as much fun and pleasure as you had when you built up your SFC from nothing.

Above all, if you do decide to expand, the pace of your expansion must be governed by the same business sense and ability to face reality which should have governed and informed every aspect of the formation of your high-income consultancy. Cultivate your business sense, never be afraid of facing the reality of your business life – even at times when facing that reality is acutely unpleasant – and you will minimise your financial risk, you will maximise your financial reward, you will make your clients happy, and you will enjoy what you do. And ultimately, it is that fundamental enjoyment of your life as a consultant which is an even greater reward for your hard work than any amount of cash can ever be.

172

Index

■

accountant, choosing an, 119–120
accounts, 60
agreements, 160–162
Amstrad PCW9512, 68
answering-machine, 70–71
Arthur Andersen, 64

bad business philosophy, 44–49
Big, 50–51
business cards, 82–83
business clothing, 85
business sense, definition of, 49–57

California, 52
Carnegie, Dale 40, 127, 142
clients, how to make them think
    you're wonderful, 121–145
competitive pitches, 164
consultancy, types of 2–3
consultant, definition of, 1
consultants, rationale for using,
    6–10
compliment slips, 81
continuation sheets, 80–81
Coopers & Lybrand, 64

Dembitz, Alex, 30, 35–36
Dickens, Charles, 136

Eastern Europe, 19–20, 30
Empire State Building, 90
equipment, choosing, 68–75
expansion, 165–172
Europe, xiv

facsimile machine (fax), 69–70
filing, 75–78
Financial Times, 76
furniture, 72–73

Growing a Business (Paul Hawken),
    40, 50, 52, 127, 136

Hamlet, 31
'hands-on' consultant, rise of, 10–12
Hanks, Tom, 50–51

Hawken, Paul, 40–41, 50, 127, 136
Hemingway, Ernest, 136
*How to Win Friends and Influence
    People* (Dale Carnegie), 40, 127,
    142

IBM, 68–69
IDOM Consultants, 30, 35–36
incremental competitive advantage,
    29
invoices, 81–82
insurance, 188–189

James Essinger Associates, 62, 139
Johnson, Doctor Samuel, 21

leasing, drawbacks of, 73–74
letterheads, 79–80
letters, 129–131, 149–157
Loggia, Roberts, 51

The Mikado, xiii
McDonalds, 37
Management Buy-Outs (MBOs) 47
McCormack, Mark, 133
meetings, 132–136
mentor, function of, 56
money, 20–21, 23–25, 86–120
    and financial hell, 89–91
    guidelines for borrowing, 92
    importance of avoiding accruing
        bad debts 109–116
    importance of making money by
        not spending it, 94–95
    importance of preoccupation with,
        87–88
    importance of starting SFC with
        minimal money, 93–94
    principles for good financial
        management, 90
motivation, 18–25

Newton, Sir Isaac, 41

personal appearance, importance of
    133–134

personal computer, 68–69
personal factors for success, 12–18
photocopier, 71–72
Polonius (in *Hamlet*), 31
Pooh-Bah (in *The Mikado*), xiii
planning your consultancy, 26–39
presentations, 162–164
pricing, 95–108
proposals, 136–138, 159–60

Reagan, President Ronald, 19
recruitment, 168–171
repetitive strain injury (RSI), 73

Schwartz, FAO, 51
Schwarzenegger, Arnold, xv
'self-fuelling consultancy,' (SFC)
        definition of, 40
setting up your consultancy, 40–85
Shorter Oxford English Dictionary,
        the, 1
Shakespeare, William, 30–31
Sinatra, Frank, 3
sole proprietorship, advantages of,
        60
sole proprietorship, possible
        disadvantages of, 60–62
spelling, importance of accurate,
        126–128
starting small and growing

organically, importance of,
        42–44
stationery, choosing, 78–84

telephone, 69–70, 125–126
Thatcher, Margaret, 47
The Sun Also Rises (Ernest
        Hemingway), 136
Touche Ross, 64
'tradeskill' 50, 52
'typos', importance of avoiding,
        129–130

Unique Selling Propositions (USPs),
        29, 45

Wall Street Journal, 76
*What They Don't Teach You at
        Harvard Business School* (Mark
        McCormack), 133
winning new business, 146–164
working from home, advantages of,
        66
working from home, supposed
        disadvantages of, 67–68
writing, guidelines for good, 30–31,
        136–137

'Yellow Pages', 149